WATERFALL HIKES
IN THE CANADIAN ROCKIES
VOL. 2: NORTH

STEVE TERSMETTE

WATERFALL
in the Canadian Rockies
HIKES

**MOUNT ROBSON · VALEMOUNT · JASPER · DAVID THOMPSON
BANFF · ICEFIELDS PARKWAY**

Volume Two

RMB

For information on purchasing bulk quantities of this book, or to obtain media excerpts or invite the author to speak at an event, please visit rmbooks.com and select the "Contact" tab.

RMB | Rocky Mountain Books Ltd.
rmbooks.com
@rmbooks
facebook.com/rmbooks

Cataloguing data available from Library and Archives Canada
ISBN 9781771606882 (softcover)
ISBN 9781771606899 (electronic)

All photographs are by Steve Tersmette unless otherwise noted.

Printed and bound in China

We would like to also take this opportunity to acknowledge the traditional territories upon which we live and work. In Calgary, Alberta, we acknowledge the Niitsítapi (Blackfoot) and the people of the Treaty 7 region in Southern Alberta, which includes the Siksika, the Piikuni, the Kainai, the Tsuut'ina and the Stoney Nakoda First Nations, including Chiniki, Bearpaw, and Wesley First Nations. The City of Calgary is also home to Métis Nation of Alberta, Region III. In Victoria, British Columbia, we acknowledge the traditional territories of the Lkwungen (Esquimalt, and Songhees), Malahat, Pacheedaht, Scia'new, T'Sou-ke and W̱SÁNEĆ (Pauquachin, Tsartlip, Tsawout, Tseycum) peoples.

We acknowledge the financial support of the Government of Canada through the Canada Book Fund and the Canada Council for the Arts, and of the province of British Columbia through the British Columbia Arts Council and the Book Publishing Tax Credit.

DISCLAIMER
The actions described in this book may be considered inherently dangerous activities. Individuals undertake these activities at their own risk. The information put forth in this guide has been collected from a variety of sources and is not guaranteed to be completely accurate or reliable. Many conditions and some information may change owing to weather and numerous other factors beyond the control of the authors and publishers. Individuals or groups must determine the risks, use their own judgment, and take full responsibility for their actions. Do not depend on any information found in this book for your own personal safety. Your safety depends on your own good judgment based on your skills, education, and experience.

It is up to the users of this guidebook to acquire the necessary skills for safe experiences and to exercise caution in potentially hazardous areas. The authors and publishers of this guide accept no responsibility for your actions or the results that occur from another's actions, choices, or judgments. If you have any doubt as to your safety or your ability to attempt anything described in this guidebook, do not attempt it.

Contents

TANGLE FALLS

Foreword

The first time I learned about Jasper National Park was on a cold winter day in late 2012. My partner and I had been offered two teaching jobs in a community that was a mere three-hour drive from this paradise, and I was researching nearby mountain parks in an attempt to broaden our Rockies experience. I had spent a ton of time in Glacier National Park, Montana, and a tiny bit in Kananaskis and Banff (living in southern Saskatchewan, it was actually quicker for us to dip down into Montana and then over to Glacier). When I looked at the descriptions of the trails and of the townsite of Jasper, the word that kept forming in my mind was *wilderness*. We decided to accept the job offers and headed to north-central Alberta, now so much closer to our beloved Rockies. Little did I know, a few years later my partner and I would get the opportunity to actually be a part of this wild mountain community of Jasper.

When we moved to Jasper in the fall of 2017, having been visiting at least twice a month since 2013, I couldn't believe our luck: our backyard now held a variety of adventures that would never be depleted. With a short drive down the parkway we could visit Athabasca, Sunwapta, Beauty Creek and Tangle Falls, just to name a few. If we ventured onto the trails we could visit seldom seen cascades such as those found on Saturday Night Lake Loop or the more epic Snake Indian Falls (my personal Jasper favourite). Although as I'm writing this, I'm reminded of the impressive cascade at Waterfall campground in South Jasper, not to mention the one you find as you descend into the Brazeau Valley from Nigel Pass, which are definitely two more favourites! Sitting and listening to the sounds of the water hit the rocks and watching the dippers fly around should be a part of everyone's "de-stress" toolkit.

I hope this book motivates you to get out on the trails, into nature, and experience the rejuvenating powers of waterfalls in Jasper's Canadian Rockies. I'm excited for the hikes that Steve will share with you, including some I've never been on, even after exploring Jasper for the past 10 years.

Yours from Jasper,
Brigid "Scrambles" Scott
@rockymountainscrambler

Diving, jumping, or kayaking into the pools or creek below Sutherland Falls is **extremely dangerous**. Most people are hurt. You assume all liability for your actions should you attempt it.

BRITISH
COLUMBIA

Introduction

I was that kid: pressed against the back window of the family van searching for roadside cascades as we made our way west for an annual summer camping trip. Every single little stream that poured out of the mountains gave rise to a backseat celebration before we reset our eyes, hoping to catch another fleeting glimpse of the next waterfall. Not much has changed. I am still that kid, although now, as the driver, it is slightly more dangerous to be on the lookout for waterfalls while negotiating the Formula One racetrack that the Trans-Canada Highway has become.

The captivating force that attracts people to waterfalls is nothing less than magical. From long silvery threads, to small hypnotic cascades delicately bubbling over rocks and tree limbs, to the deafening roar of a swollen river rocketing over a cliff, people go to great lengths to seek out these natural wonders. Waterfalls provide an escape, a solace for the mind while soothing the soul. And, they are pretty things to photograph.

The purpose of this book is to provide a simple, family-friendly hiking guide as an aid in locating and accessing the spectacular waterfalls in the Canadian Rockies. This comprehensive guide details more than seventy waterfalls in the Alberta and BC Rockies encompassing an area north of the Trans-Canada Highway to Valemount and includes the many iconic national and provincial parks that straddle the Continental Divide.

After completion of the first installment in this series, *Waterfall Hikes in Southern British Columbia*, my wife and children operated under the assumption that they would receive a respite from the relentless day-hiking and waterfall exploration. They were terribly mistaken! Early on in the reconnaissance for *Waterfall Hikes in the Canadian Rockies*, it became immediately clear that a single guide would not be adequate and the book was divided into two volumes, North and South, which further prolonged my family's involvement in this project. Thank you to my far better half, Katie, and our kids, Hanna and Jasper, for both their enthusiasm and their patience while we continued to set our sights on the numerous hikes that pepper the Canadian Rockies.

I owe a debt of gratitude to Adam Sawyer (Professional Gentleman of Leisure) for inspiring me to get writing and for the idea of creating these guidebooks. Thanks to my good friend Robin, sister-in-law Tawny and RMB editor extraordinaire Joe Wilderson for reading, re-reading and surgically editing draft after draft of both this volume and its predecessor. To my parents for instilling in me a deep-seated and insatiable love for the mountains, hiking and the outdoors. To my many partners in adventure over the years who continue to fuel my passion and whose own accomplishments never cease to amaze. To Meghan Ward at Crowfoot Media for giving me a shot. To Brigid Scott for enthusiastically providing the foreword for this book. And finally to Don Gorman and the fine team at Rocky Mountain Books for their support for this project. Their guidance, professionalism and flexibility have been critical for bringing these books to fruition. Thank you!

Writing this book not only kept our family hiking and exploring together but also filled a clear void in the guidebook genre: kid-friendly exploration. Oh, and did I mention it's about waterfalls?!

Using the guidebook

This is a comprehensive, simple and family-friendly hiking guide that assists readers in locating and accessing the spectacular waterfalls of the Canadian Rockies. While every measure has been taken to ensure the accuracy of driving and hiking directions, even the most competent of writers have mashed buttons on their keyboard at some point. If you notice an error, please inform the author and publisher so that potential future printings and editions can be updated.

Are there more waterfalls to be found? Yes, and I happened upon many that are not included in this book for a variety of reasons. First and foremost, I wanted to produce a responsible and ethical guide that did not encourage off-trail use, especially in the national and provincial parks. For safety's sake, a number of hikes were omitted due to excessive bushwhacking or unsafe river crossings. Lastly, I did not want to promote hikes where the access may be infringing on private property. I hope you as the user will employ these same ethics and standards in your explorations. So let's get to it!

Trail difficulty ratings

You'll find a variety of trails described here, from five-minute walks away from your car to destinations that may require a night out in a tent. Difficulty ratings are highly subjective and depend on the reader's experience, comfort and fitness level. The trails are rated with a family in mind, including younger children that can walk on a hiking trail on their own. My kids were nine and eleven years old during the construction of this guidebook and therefore serve as the measuring stick for hiking times and difficulty. Read trail descriptions carefully to assess whether a hike may or may not be within your wheelhouse. The reader is responsible for assessing their own capabilities and conditions to ensure they are selecting hikes suited to their skill level.

Trail difficulty can vary depending on conditions, time of day, season, weather, precipitation and temperature. Hike at your own risk and make smart decisions based on your skill level and experience. Even hiking on well-used trails has its hazards such as roots, rocks and mud. Another thing to keep in mind is that waterfalls tend to get things pretty wet. Spray can travel dozens of metres, making the areas around waterfalls slippery and dangerous, even with good footwear.

- Easy Less than half a day. One-way distance of less than 4 km or 1.5 hours on well-defined and well-marked trails with relatively minor elevation gains.
- Moderate A half-day to a full-day hike. Between 4 km and 7 km one-way with modest elevation gains or undulating terrain. May include shorter hikes with sustained steep or narrow sections.
- Difficult Requires a long day or an overnight trip. May have significant elevation gains. Potential hazards may include difficult-to-follow trails, creek crossings or steep terrain. Pay careful attention to trail descriptions.

Hiking times and distances provided are one-way.

Getting there

While most trails in this guide are readily accessible from a highway, some areas, especially around the Forestry Trunk Road and near Nordegg, are accessible only by resource or forestry service roads (FSRs). Some resource roads are well maintained for industrial or recreational purposes while others fall into disrepair or go years without the benefit of maintenance. Access difficulty is described for a two-wheel-drive vehicle. If a four-wheel-drive is recommended or required, this is noted in the driving directions and the access is classified as Difficult.

- Easy Access and parking via a paved road.
- Moderate Access and parking via a well-maintained FSR or other unpaved road. No concerns with the use of a two-wheel-drive vehicle.
- Difficult Access via an unmaintained backcountry road. Four-wheel drive may be recommended or even necessary. Pay close attention to driving directions and noted hazards.

It should be noted that our two vehicles had minor discrepancies in their odometer readings between waypoints. This may result in slight variances between the actual distance and the information provided. As much as possible, a landmark is provided with each distance to ensure access descriptions are as accurate as possible.

SAFETY ON RESOURCE ROADS

Forestry service roads are typically one- or two-lane gravel roads built for industrial purposes and used to access natural resources in remote areas. They are used primarily by vehicles engaged in forestry, mining, oil and gas or agriculture. In addition to industrial access, resource roads are used by both the general public and commercial operators such as backcountry skiing or hunting businesses, lodges or other accommodation providers. FSRs serve as crucial links for rural communities and access to recreational opportunities.

As they are not built or maintained to the same standards as public highways, resource roads can be rough, with narrow gravel surfaces. There may be roadside brush limiting visibility, soft shoulders, more curves, tighter curves and much steeper grades than encountered on public highways. These roads do not necessarily have signs or barriers identifying all hazards or dangers. Common dangers include large industrial vehicles; high traffic volume; poor visibility due to brush, alignment, dust, fog or smoke; passing or being passed on narrow roads; changing road surface conditions; weather; wildlife and so forth. A radio is recommended on resource roads that are actively being using for forestry or mining. It is also a good idea to drive with your headlights on to improve your own visibility.

Resource road users must drive with an abundance of caution at all times!

Waterfall safety

Waterfalls are incredibly beautiful but can be incredibly dangerous. In the age of smart phone, social media and the selfie, more and more people are taking risks to get The Shot. Most of these safety tips should be common sense but, you know what they say about common sense!

1. Stay on established trails. Not only does deviating from trails destroy vegetation but undeveloped terrain can be highly unstable. Hiking off trail may put others below you at risk as soil or rocks can be knocked loose.

2. Don't swim or cross creeks above waterfalls. One wrong step or a strong current can take you from the top of a waterfall to the bottom in a split second. Some locations have designated viewing areas or fencing to restrict access to dangerous or unstable areas. These fences, guards and railings are in place for your safety.

3. Don't. Jump. Off. Waterfalls. Period. There are so many factors to consider including water depth, currents and rocks or debris below the surface. Pools can change year to year, even season to season with runoff carrying rocks, logs and debris downstream. Water levels change seasonally and can also be affected by rainfall. Never assume a pool is safe. People have died at some of the waterfalls in this very book. Again: don't jump off waterfalls.

4. Avoid rocks and climbing at the base of waterfalls. Spray and mist from waterfalls make rocks and trails slippery, especially near the pools at the base of falls.

5. Watch for streamflow advisories (usually posted during spring runoff). Water can rise up over established trails or creek crossings. The higher volume in the spring creates fast-moving water, debris flows and bank erosion. Streamflow can increase as much as fifteen times the normal volume, especially during periods of rapid melting, after rainstorms and high runoff.

6. Wear appropriate footwear. A good pair of light hikers are essential for most routes. Trails may be slippery, especially as you approach waterfalls. If you need to cross a creek, best to have a pair of water shoes or a full-coverage sandal that can be secured to your foot at the top and back (read: flip flops are not appropriate footwear).

Hiking with kids

One of the biggest hurdles we faced as new parents was to find a variety of short, easy, child-friendly hikes. Most of the hiking guides currently in publication describe breathtaking vistas, shimmering mountain lakes and, without a doubt, some of the highest-value scenery in the world. Many are lengthy day hikes. Some involve backcountry camping. Most include substantial elevation gain. Like many parents we transitioned from baby wraps to kid carriers to hand holding or to simply carrying kids in our arms. Some days were hugely successful, while other days were nothing short of torturous. The one thing we craved was to have more options to transition our kids from our backs to the trails.

As a father of two I can say my biggest fault was expecting too much from my kids at too young an age. Fortunately, I did not break them completely. So, having learned the lesson myself, the most important wisdom I can pass along is this: be patient. When patience fails, however, here are a few tips to keep kids keen on hiking.

1. Make sure they're comfortable. It might mean bringing an extra jacket, pants, toques, mitts, socks, hats and undies. If a child isn't comfortable, don't expect them to hike with you.
2. Arm yourself with games to play such as I Spy, 20 Questions, riddles or just plain old silly facts and useless information. If a child isn't interested, don't expect them to hike with you.
3. Bring snacks and take breaks. Yes, I agree that being asked to take a break five minutes from the car is annoying and I'll leave it up to you to decide how reasonable the stop-for-a-snack request is but, if a child is hungry, don't expect them to hike with you.
4. Pick hikes that are within your kids' ability and comfort level. While carefully pushing my own children in an effort to help them grow, I would never advocate for doing something unsafe. There is also a discernible difference between comfort and safety. If a child feels unsafe, don't expect them to hike with you.
5. Take a camera. No, not for you. For the kids. Taking photos gives kids a sense of purpose and achievement. They can see the results immediately; it gives them a task and keeps their interest up. Celebrate the little victories, whether it's as simple as taking a good photo or completing an easy hike. If a child doesn't feel like they've accomplished something, don't expect them to hike to with you.
6. Bring candy.

My children asked if they could provide some tips from their perspective as well. So, in no particular order:

1. "Just because an adult thinks they're right, doesn't mean they're right. Didn't you bring a map?"
2. "We're lost, aren't we."
3. "Ummmm, dad... kids don't really like bushwhacking."
4. "If we ask 'Are we there yet?', just say we're close."
5. "Bring candy."

Leave No Trace

If you're like me, finding garbage in the backcountry puts you in a bad mood. And it's not just the garbage. I despise braided trails and shortcuts on switchbacks. I shudder when I happen upon random fire rings, and cringe when I see cairns that have no purpose. The Leave No Trace principles are critical to preserving the outdoor experience, and it is never too early to familiarize yourself with backcountry etiquette. If you consider yourself a pro in this regard, pass your knowledge along to teach the next generation of trail stewards!

THE 7 PRINCIPLES OF LEAVE NO TRACE

1. Plan ahead and prepare
2. Travel and camp on durable surfaces
3. Dispose of waste properly
4. Leave what you find
5. Minimize campfire impacts
6. Respect wildlife
7. Be considerate of other visitors

For more information visit **leavenotrace.ca**

It is important to note that dogs must be leashed when hiking in all national and provincial parks. If your furry friends tag along for the hike, keep them leashed and under control at all times and pick up after your dogs (including disposing of the bag afterwards).

Wildlife

What would a guidebook be without speaking about wildlife? Let's face it, this is their backyard and we are guests, so give wildlife a wide berth. You can encounter all sorts of woodland creatures at any time and without warning, including everything from ground squirrels and deer to porcupines, rattlesnakes, foxes and bears. While the discussion about an animal such as a chipmunk is limited mostly to "don't feed the chipmunks," the pep talk on an apex predator such as a grizzly bear is a slightly different chat. It is also one that warrants precious space on paper.

Bears

While bears generally tend to avoid people, encounters do happen. The best preparation is knowledge: knowing how to avoid an encounter and knowing what to do in case of an encounter. Avoiding one altogether is the best idea. Take precautions such as travelling in larger groups, making lots of noise and keeping dogs on leashes. Watch for fresh markings such as scat, tracks, overturned rocks and torn up logs. If you come across a dead animal, leave the area and report the carcass to a conservation officer or park staff. Carry bear spray, keep it easily accessible and know how to use it.

If you do encounter a bear, stay calm and have your bear spray ready to use. Speak to the bear in a firm voice. Make yourself appear as large as possible and back away slowly. Stay together in your group and pick up small children. If you're carrying a backpack, leave it on. Either wait for the bear to move on, give it a wide berth or slowly back away and leave the area. Report encounters to a conservation officer or Parks staff.

If the bear escalates its behaviour and charges, be prepared and use your bear spray. If the bear attacks and makes contact, play dead by lying on your stomach with your hands over the back of your neck. However, if the attack continues for more than two minutes, fight back. We recommend reading other resources on bear safety. The more knowledge you have about bear behaviour, avoiding encounters and using bear spray, the better prepared you will be in bear country. Parks Canada and WildSafeBC both have excellent information available for free (see the Online Resources list at the back of the book).

As a wise co-captain of the Waterton Shoreline Cruise Company once said: "Make some noise. This is their home. The least we can do is ring the doorbell to let them know we're here."

Mosquitos

Mossies, bloodsuckers, vampires... merchants of death!! In addition to being hugely annoying, these insects can make being in the outdoors aggravating in certain locations. Even at elevations where their presence may be confusing, they are looking for a meal and will certainly find you. If you're outdoors in the Canadian Rockies, you are in mosquito country. Even if you personally feel you can tough it out, for the sake of your children, bring bug spray.

ADDITIONAL NOTES ON WILDLIFE

The primary objective when it comes to wildlife conflicts while recreating outdoors is to reduce the opportunities for encounters altogether. The best thing you can do is arm yourself with knowledge. Know what types of wildlife you can expect to come across and how to deal with a direct encounter. Be vigilant with food and garbage. Animals that are fed become habituated to human interactions and the chances of conflicts with animals become much higher.

Logistics and planning

It's important to note that the majority of these hikes are located within a national park, where you'll need a parks pass to stop, park and utilize parks infrastructure. Passes can be purchased at park gates at the entry points to Jasper and Banff national parks. They are also available at visitor centres and through some online outlets. For hikes located outside a national park, passes are not required in any other location, including Alberta or British Columbia provincial parks.

Frontcountry camping locations generally offer a limited number of first-come, first-served sites, although reservations are highly recommended to avoid disappointment. Backcountry camping requires a permit and reservations in all national parks and most provincial parks, usually obtained at the time of booking. Random camping is generally not permitted unless on Crown land, with some exceptions in provincial wildland areas.

For park pass, camping and reservation information, contact the appropriate powers that be. We have compiled a useful list of contacts and resources in the back of this guidebook.

HIKING SEASONS

Many trails in this book are accessible year-round, and each season brings with it a unique beauty as well as a different set of conditions and hazards.

In the springtime, especially later in the season, streams will start to become swollen with runoff from the melting snowpack. Spring is generally also the rainy season in the mountains, which can cause unexpected surges in water levels. Expect damp, muddy or even snow-covered trails.

With swift streamflow and high water, creek crossings can be dangerous or even impossible. Stay back from banks, as fast-moving water can cause them to erode and potentially collapse without warning. It is also advisable to pack warm layers and extra socks.

In the summertime, the streams return to their normal rate of flow. The summer months will also bring hot temperatures and insects. Pack plenty of water, even on short hikes. Remember your sunscreen and bug repellent.

Autumn is a beautiful time to tackle waterfall hikes. The change in season brings a rich palette of colour to the scene, in addition to cooler and insect-free days. These days are also shorter and can cool off quickly. Frost may be present on trails early in the day and snow is a common occurrence, even in September. Remember to pack layers, an extra jacket and even a headlamp, especially if you're starting a hike later in the day.

Winter brings the most dramatic change to the landscape. Many waterfalls will partially freeze, while others will ice over completely. When hiking in the wintertime it is critically important to wear warm clothes, even on sunny days, as hypothermia can set in quickly. Wear a toque and warm gloves; an extra pair is a great idea. Expect trails to be snowbound and slippery. Hiking poles and microspikes for footwear are strongly recommended. For longer day hikes you may want to consider packing a warm drink in a thermos. When hiking in the winter it is imperative to consider the avalanche risk in some locations. If you are in doubt as to whether or not a route is safe, or you do not have the appropriate training, avoid the situation altogether.

A QUICK NOTE ON WATERFALL NAMES

For the most part, the names of waterfalls given are their official names as recognized on mapping sources such as Natural Resources Canada, national or provincial park maps, or a published name as per other literature and guides. If there is no official or recognized name, the name of the watercourse is referenced along with a notation that this is an unofficial name. Some waterfalls have been christened with a variety of names that may be used locally rather than officially. To avoid confusion, where waterfalls have been referred to by more than one name, their alias will be listed in the description.

CREDITS

All photographs are by the author unless noted otherwise.

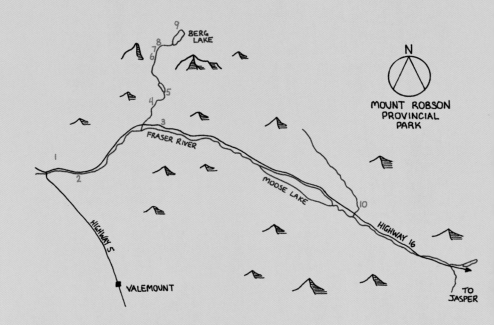

9
8
7
6
BERG
LAKE

5
4
3
FRASER RIVER

1
2

HIGHWAY 5

VALEMOUNT

MOOSE LAKE

10

HIGHWAY 16

TO
JASPER

N

MOUNT ROBSON
PROVINCIAL
PARK

CHAPTER 1

Mount Robson Provincial Park to Valemount

If some of the premier hiking in the country beneath the tallest mountain in the Canadian Rockies isn't enough to whet your appetite, how about an assortment of spectacular waterfalls? With hiking options from short, easy strolls to overnight trips on the famed Berg Lake trail, there are options for every age and experience level. Many of the hikes in the park are concentrated around the Mount Robson visitor centre beneath the towering mass of the nearly 4000-metre mountain. The parking area and trailheads are an 85 km drive (60 minutes) from Jasper, AB, or a 37 km drive (25 minutes) from Valemount, BC. Driving distances are given from the junction of Highways 93 and 16 near Jasper.

Mount Robson Provincial Park is bisected by Highway 16, which is a thoroughfare for vacationers and truckers travelling between central Alberta and central British Columbia. The route is also a critical link for residents and workers from the towns of Valemount and Jasper.

It is important to note that there is no cell service in the park. Ensure you leave a detailed itinerary with a friend or family member, along with your estimated time to check in or return home. Satellite messengers are a useful tool for communicating in remote areas without cellular reception.

Berg Lake day-use pass: In 2020, six provincial parks in BC introduced a day-use permit system to help manage the heavy visitation these parks experience. Mount Robson Provincial Park is one of these, as a free day-use pass is now required for access to the Berg Lake trail. These passes may be reserved online in advance through the BC Parks camping reservations webpage or at the Mount Robson visitor centre. You must carry your pass at all times while hiking Berg Lake Trail. Dogs are permitted on leash for day-hiking to Kinney Lake only; they are not allowed beyond Kinney Lake or overnight

RAINBOW CANYON

on Berg Lake Trail. If hiking with your dog, bring a bag and always pick up after them.

Note: In early July 2021, the Robson River flooded with high temperatures and a sudden melt of the snowpack at higher elevation. The resulting rise in water along the Berg Lake trail resulted in excessive trail and infrastructure damage including destruction of bridges, pathways and campsites. The trail was subsequently closed for the remainder of the 2021 and 2022 seasons with a full reopening of the famed route targeted for summer 2025. At the time of writing, the trail descriptions reflected conditions prior to the flood.

For more information contact the Mount Robson Provincial Park visitor centre:

bcparks.ca/explore/parkpgs/mt_robson/
Highway 16, Mount Robson, V0E 2Z0
(250) 566-4038
Camping reservations: 1-800-689-9025 or visit
camping.bcparks.ca

1. L'estrange Creek Falls

LOCATION: Little Lost Lake Recreation Site, Valemount, BC
DRIVING DIFFICULTY: Easy
HIKING DIFFICULTY: Moderate (due to elevation gain and trail grade)
HIKING DISTANCE: 2.3 km
HIKING TIME: 1 h

Blink while you're driving and you might miss this hike entirely. Located just outside the Mount Robson Provincial Park boundary, and without the benefit of a signed parking area, this gorgeous route is easy to overlook. But it's an amazing spot that features creeks, waterfalls, a lake, old-growth forest and an abundance of solitude.

Driving directions

From the junction of Highways 93 and 16 near Jasper, drive west on Highway 16 for 99.5 km. Pass through a set of yellow gates and park in a large, unsigned pullout on the left-hand (south) side of the highway.

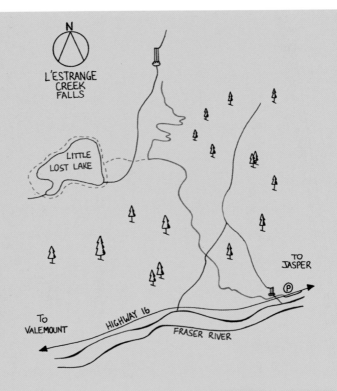

Hiking directions

From the parking area, cross the highway carefully and walk west on the shoulder for 100 m. (You will walk by another waterfall concealed among the trees above the road.) Locate a trail in the ditch that ascends into the trees with a brown Rec Site sign for Little Lost Lake. Hike this well-used trail through old-growth cedar, fir and cottonwood trees to a trail junction at 1.4 km (signs for "Trail" and "Waterfall"). Stay right. From here the trail ascends steeply above Little Lost Lake via a series of switchbacks. At 2.1 km stay left at a nondescript junction (the right-hand trail heads for a lookout). At this point the

trail gets even steeper as it approaches the waterfall. Step with care; the steep, side-sloping trail near the falls is quite exposed.

While not a long hike, this trail gains nearly 400 metres of elevation from the parking area to the falls, hence the Moderate rating.

More to explore: Little Lost Lake

From the trail junction at 1.4 km, instead of ascending to the waterfall, you can continue straight on the main pathway for a couple hundred metres to Little Lost Lake. Giant cottonwood and fir trees ring the small lake. A lesser-used trail continues along the lakeshore. This makes a nice addition to the waterfall hike and a great lunch spot on the return trip.

Note: My trip here included what can only be described as a tactical, well-planned and well-executed ambush by the mosquitos that inhabit these woods. While I managed to remain relatively unscathed during our foray in and out, my family did not fare so well and continue to hold this against me. Be a better parent than I was and pack bug spray for the sake of your marriage and children.

2. Rearguard Falls

LOCATION: Rearguard Falls Provincial Park, Valemount, BC
DRIVING DIFFICULTY: Easy
HIKING DIFFICULTY: Easy
HIKING DISTANCE: 350 m
HIKING TIME: 10 min

Rearguard Falls is a short waterfall but what it lacks in height it makes up for with the staggering volume of water that passes over it. The falls are especially impressive during spring runoff. Although the headwaters of the Fraser River are more than a hundred kilometres away, the river expands greatly as it collects other creeks, streams and rivers along the way. By the time it reaches Rearguard Falls, the Fraser has attained "mighty-river" status, the water becoming so turbulent here that it effectively halts the ability of salmon to travel any farther upstream.

Driving directions

From the junction of Highways 93 and 16 near Jasper, drive west on Highway 16 for 97.3 km. The parking area for Rearguard Falls is on the left-hand (south) side of the highway and is well signed.

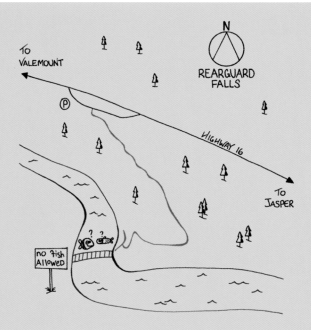

Hiking directions

From the parking area, follow a broad pathway that descends to the Fraser River. There are multiple viewpoints protected by guardrails and fencing. The trail ends at a large viewing platform above the falls. In the spring and early summer, the spray from the falls will make everything near the river soggy, including the pathways, the surrounding trees and the surrounding people.

Salmon and the mighty Fraser

It is a 1260-kilometre aquatic expedition from the Pacific Ocean to Rearguard Falls. The vast majority of chinook salmon that make their annual migration up the Fraser River will ultimately end their trip here. Only the strongest fish are able to negotiate the falls and continue upstream. The chinook salmon (also known as king salmon) are the largest of the Pacific salmon species, weigh on average 14 kg and are valued by both anglers and the seafood industry.

3. Overlander Falls

LOCATION: Mount Robson Provincial Park, BC
DRIVING DIFFICULTY: Easy
HIKING DIFFICULTY: Easy
HIKING DISTANCE: 550 m
HIKING TIME: 10 min

The gentle jaunt to Overlander Falls is a great starter hike with small children or a nice alternative if the parking area is overflowing at the Mount Robson visitor centre. The falls are named for a group of prospectors from Ontario that were travelling to BC's Cariboo region in search of gold. The Overlanders passed by this location in 1862. At the time, the usual route to British Columbia was by sailing around South America.

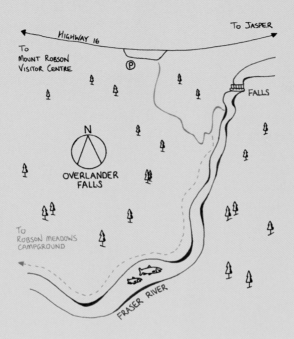

Driving directions

From the junction of Highways 93 and 16 near Jasper, drive west on Highway 16 for 83.7 km. The parking area for Overlander Falls is on the left-hand (south) side of the highway and is signed.

Hiking directions

From the parking area, follow a wide pathway through the densely treed forest that descends to a viewpoint along the Fraser River below Overlander Falls. The viewing area is protected by guardrails.

Alternative access trail

From the Robson Meadows campground, a 2.5 km trail follows alongside the Fraser River to the east with views down into the Fraser River canyon. Starting at the campground, walk down Hargreaves Road toward the river and locate a signed trail for Overlander Falls.

4. Knowlton Falls

LOCATION: Mount Robson Provincial Park, BC
DRIVING DIFFICULTY: Easy
HIKING DIFFICULTY: Easy
HIKING DISTANCE: 2.2 km
HIKING TIME: 40 min

Knowlton Falls is the first (albeit obscure) waterfall that hikers will encounter on the Berg Lake trail and it's easily overlooked by those hell-bent on the more notable destinations farther up the valley. If you're short on time, hiking with little ones or just need to stretch your legs, this is a simple and straightforward objective near the highway.

Driving directions

From the junction of Highways 93 and 16 near Jasper, drive west on Highway 16 for 85 km to the Mount Robson Provincial Park visitor centre. Turn right off the highway and follow the road for an additional kilometre to the Berg Lake trailhead.

Hiking directions

From the trailhead, follow the well-signed Berg Lake trail for 2.2 km. Knowlton Falls is a small waterfall on the Robson River which may be substantially submerged during periods of high streamflow or spring runoff. At the time of writing, the condition of the waterfall was unknown due to the recent flooding and permanent alterations of the Robson River.

Know before you go

Since spring 2020, the Berg Lake trail has been on the day-use-permit program. Reservations for any of the campgrounds along the trail will automatically include the trail permit for the dates reserved. Day hikers must obtain their permit from the visitor centre on the day of use, starting at 8:00 a.m., or reserve one ahead of time.

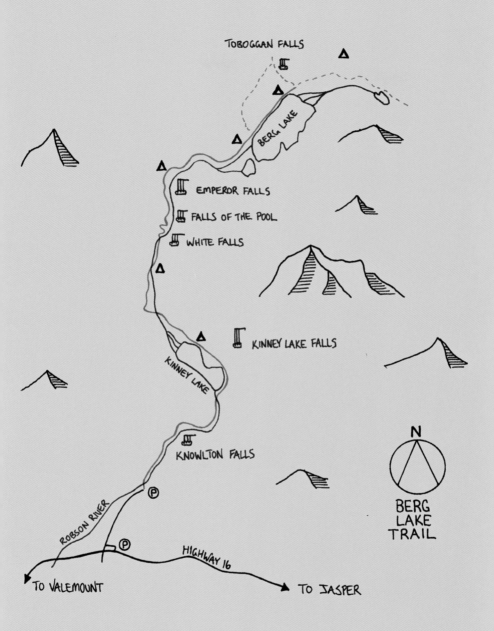

TOBOGGAN FALLS

BERG LAKE

EMPEROR FALLS

FALLS OF THE POOL

WHITE FALLS

KINNEY LAKE FALLS

KINNEY LAKE

KNOWLTON FALLS

N

BERG LAKE TRAIL

ROBSON RIVER

HIGHWAY 16

TO VALEMOUNT

TO JASPER

5. Kinney Lake Falls

LOCATION: Mount Robson Provincial Park, BC
DRIVING DIFFICULTY: Easy
HIKING DIFFICULTY: Easy
HIKING DISTANCE: 6.9 km
HIKING TIME: 2.5 h

Driving directions

From the junction of Highways 93 and 16 near Jasper, drive west on Highway 16 for 85 km to the Mount Robson Provincial Park visitor centre. Turn right off the highway and follow the road for an additional kilometre to the Berg Lake trailhead.

Hiking directions

From the trailhead, follow the well-signed Berg Lake trail for 7 km to a shelter at the Kinney Lake campground. Kinney Lake Falls plummets down the steep flanks of Mount Robson high above the trail along the lakeshore. The falls are best viewed from the main trail about 100 metres before reaching the shelter at the campground. The trail is mainly flat to Kinney Lake, save for a couple brief inclines.

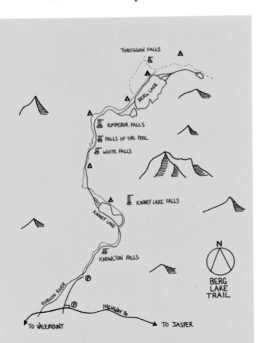

Know before you go

Bikes are permitted on the Berg Lake trail for the first 7 km to the Kinney Lake campground. This is one of the few trails in the park that allows for bicycle use. There is a bike rack at the north end of Kinney Lake to dismount and lock bicycles if proceeding farther on foot.

6. White Falls

LOCATION: Mount Robson Provincial Park, BC
DRIVING DIFFICULTY: Easy
HIKING DIFFICULTY: Moderate (overnight recommended)
HIKING DISTANCE: 12.1 km
HIKING TIME: 4–5 h

White Falls is the first "big one" on the Berg Lake trail. This multi-tiered waterfall steps down a total of 120 metres in four segments, although the topmost portion is obscured from view.

Driving directions

From the junction of Highways 93 and 16 near Jasper, drive west on Highway 16 for 85 km to the Mount Robson Provincial Park visitor centre. Turn right off the highway and follow the road for an additional kilometre to the Berg Lake trailhead.

Hiking directions

From the trailhead, follow the well-signed Berg Lake trail for 7 km to the Kinney Lake campground. Continue along the main trail past the campground and beyond the flats past the lake. At 8.5 km the trail begins a moderate but steady ascent. The Whitehorn campground is located at 11.0 km. A short spur off the main trail at 12.0 km leads to the base of White Falls.

Know before you go

The Whitehorn campground makes for an excellent first night out for backpackers heading to Berg Lake for an extended trip. The trailhead is a reasonable half-day drive from many places, such as Calgary, Edmonton or Kamloops, followed by a straightforward hike of only 11 km to Whitehorn. From there, it is a much more casual second day to the campgrounds in the vicinity of Berg Lake.

7. Falls of the Pool

LOCATION: Mount Robson Provincial Park, BC
DRIVING DIFFICULTY: Easy
HIKING DIFFICULTY: Moderate (overnight recommended)
HIKING DISTANCE: 13.2 km
HIKING TIME: 4.0 h

The Falls of the Pool is another great trailside attraction on the way to Berg Lake. With the trail high above the Robson River at this point, you are rewarded with a bird's-eye view of another one of Mount Robson's larger waterfalls.

Driving directions

From the junction of Highways 93 and 16 near Jasper, drive west on Highway 16 for 85 km to the Mount Robson Provincial Park visitor centre. Turn right off the highway and follow the road for an additional kilometre to the Berg Lake trailhead.

Hiking directions

From the trailhead, follow the well-signed Berg Lake trail for 7 km to the Kinney Lake campground. Continue along the main trail, past the campground and beyond the flats on the other side of the lake. At 8.5 km the trail begins a moderate but steady ascent. The Whitehorn campground is located at 11.0 km. The lookout above Falls of the Pool is located along the trail at 13.2 km.

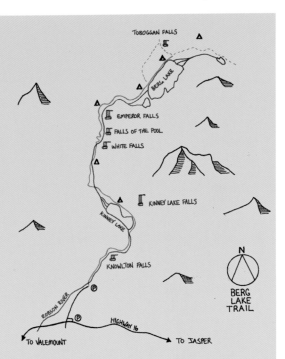

The Valley of a Thousand Falls

As you hike beyond Kinney Lake, the large gravel outwash marks the entrance to what is known as the Valley of a Thousand Falls. Besides the very large and impressive cascades along the Robson River, a number of tall, narrow ones cling to the steep flanks of both Whitehorn Mountain and Mount Robson, which form the valley.

8. Emperor Falls

LOCATION: Mount Robson Provincial Park, BC
DRIVING DIFFICULTY: Easy
HIKING DIFFICULTY: Moderate (overnight required)
HIKING DISTANCE: 15.4 km
HIKING TIME: 5–6 h

If you walked up to this waterfall without knowing anything about the area, you might even be creative enough to come up with the name Emperor Falls on your very own. This thundering juggernaut of a cataract roars with unbridled enthusiasm as it poses in the shadow of the highest mountain in the Canadian Rockies. You'll hear it long before you see it (and may get wet from it before you see it, too). Its trademark "rooster tail" is a feature that makes this waterfall instantly recognizable.

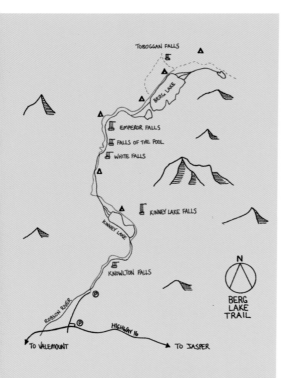

Driving directions

From the junction of Highways 93 and 16 near Jasper, drive west on Highway 16 for 85 km to the Mount Robson Provincial Park visitor centre. Turn right off the highway and follow the road for an additional kilometre to the Berg Lake trailhead.

Hiking directions

From the trailhead, follow the well-signed Berg Lake trail for 7 km to the Kinney Lake campground. Continue along the main trail past the campground and beyond the flats past the lake. At 8.5 km the trail begins a moderate but steady ascent. The Whitehorn campground is located at 11.0 km. Pass the viewpoints for White Falls and Falls of the Pool at 12.1 km and 13.2 km respectively and then continue the ascent to the impressive Emperor Falls at 15.4 km.

The Emperor's new name

Mount Robson Provincial Park was created in 1913, the same year the legendary Conrad Kain made the first ascent of the peak. Emperor Falls had already received its name two years before, during an A.O. Wheeler expedition into the region when Wheeler christened the prominent waterfall, although the name wasn't formally adopted until 1951.

PHOTO: SHAWNA AND DAMIEN RICHARD, ALPENGLOW PHOTO

9. Toboggan Falls

LOCATION: Mount Robson Provincial Park, BC
DRIVING DIFFICULTY: Easy
HIKING DIFFICULTY: Difficult (due to distance; overnight recommended)
HIKING DISTANCE: 22 km (1 km from Berg Lake campground)
HIKING TIME: 30 min from Berg Lake campground, 7–8 h from trailhead

Toboggan Falls is a popular day trip once you've made your basecamp near Berg Lake. It can be easily combined with the Mumm Basin and the Hargreaves Lake hikes, although the falls are quickly overshadowed by the high-elevation views of Mount Robson and Berg Lake. Poor little waterfall...

Driving directions

From the junction of Highways 93 and 16 near Jasper, drive west on Highway 16 for 85 km to the Mount Robson Provincial Park visitor centre. Turn right off the highway and follow the road for an additional kilometre to the Berg Lake trailhead.

Hiking directions

From the Berg Lake trailhead, follow the well-signed Berg Lake trail for 7 km to the Kinney Lake campground. At 8.5 km, after the flats beyond the lake, the trail starts to climb moderately but steadily before levelling out at the Emperor Falls campground at 16.0 km. From there, wander along the outwash path of Berg Lake before following the shoreline to the Berg Lake campground at 22.0 km.

Once at the Berg Lake campground, locate a trail behind the Hargreaves shelter that ascends steeply alongside a small creek. Toboggan Falls is located about 1.0 km up this trail.

More to explore

Berg Lake is the ultimate Rockies basecamp. Most parties will spend multiple nights here and take in the many day hikes that start from this point. The Toboggan Falls and Hargreaves Lake loop is only one option, a 6.0 km circuit that climbs to vistas high above Berg Lake. Other great options are Snowbird Pass (a 22 km, 6–8 h out and back hike), a stroll to the toe of Robson Glacier (6 km, 2–3 h), and Mumm Basin (a strenuous 7 km, 3–5 h loop that ascends steeply from the campground).

10. *Rainbow Canyon*

LOCATION: Mount Robson Provincial Park, BC
DRIVING DIFFICULTY: Moderate
HIKING DIFFICULTY: Easy
HIKING DISTANCE: 350 m
HIKING TIME: 10 min

Rainbow Canyon along the Moose River is a spectacular feature that has garnered absolutely zero fanfare, for reasons unexplained. Yet, in the early 1900s, its existence was well documented by explorers and photographers of the day. No longer will this outstanding waterfall be relegated to the archives of Canadian Rockies history! No longer will Rainbow Canyon be a simple side note on an outdated topographic map! See for yourself what folks were raving about over a hundred years ago.

Driving directions

From the junction of Highways 93 and 16 near Jasper, drive west on Highway 16 for 53 km. Cross over the Moose River and turn right off

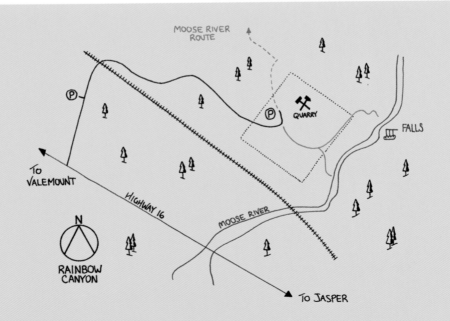

the highway onto an unsigned gravel road. Cross the railway tracks (400 m from highway), then stay right. Continue for 800 m to the Moose River trailhead, located in a decommissioned rock quarry (complete with BC Parks trailhead kiosk, outhouse and horse corral).

Hiking directions

From the Moose River trailhead, follow an old road counter-clockwise around the quarry for 300 m to a turnaround at the top of the quarry (signs for "no camping" and "no fires"). The waterfall can be heard from here. Locate a flagged trail entering the trees and follow for 50 metres to a lookout at the top of the waterfall in Rainbow Canyon. Expect to get wet, as the spray from this waterfall is spectacular. It also means the trail near the top of the falls is generally wet, muddy and slippery.

Water, water everywhere!

As you drive along the Yellowhead Highway from Jasper to Valemount, there are literally waterfalls all around. Very few of these are named and even fewer are accessible by the human form. One such waterfall is across and high above Moose Lake and is visible from the highway (you'll know it when you see it – wink, wink). This behemoth is called Thunder Falls, for obvious reasons, and can only be reached by the most ambitious of waterfall hunters after paddling across the lake and bushwhacking up steep forested slopes under the falls. Perhaps best viewed from a roadside pullout with a pair of binoculars.

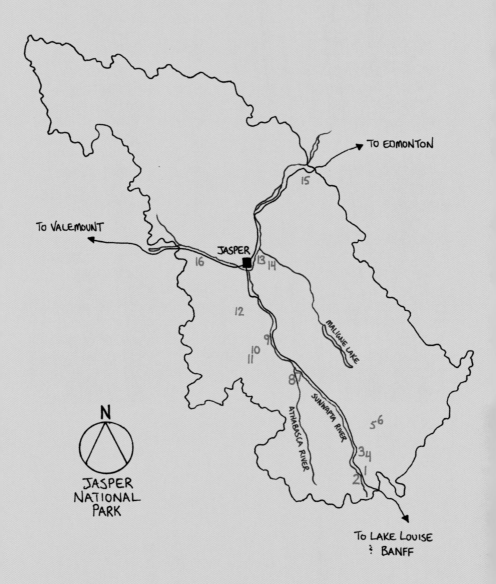

TO EDMONTON

TO VALEMOUNT

JASPER

15

16

13 14

12

MALIGNE LAKE

9

10

11

8

ATHABASCA RIVER

SUNWAPTA RIVER

5 6

3 4

1

2

N

JASPER
NATIONAL
PARK

TO LAKE LOUISE
& BANFF

CHAPTER 2

Jasper National Park

At the south end of Jasper National Park sits the greatest mass of glaciation and concentration of high mountains in the Canadian Rockies. To the north, the postcard town of Jasper. In between the two are views that will leave your jaw sore, your eyes wide and your neck rubbery. Massive glaciers cap towering peaks, and shimmering lakes reflect pristine forests along the way. For those willing to venture beyond the highway, there is an endless supply of places to explore.

Two main highways provide travel through the park: from north to south is Highway 93 and from east to west is Highway 16. The park can be accessed from three directions: from the south via Banff National Park, the Icefields Parkway and Highway 93; from the west via Valemount, BC, and Highway 16; and from the east via Hinton, AB, and Highway 16. The town of Jasper is the main service hub and offers gas, food, accommodation and visitor services.

Frontcountry and backcountry camping opportunities are abundant here, but reservable sites fill up quickly when bookings open for the season. There are alternative accommodation options, including alpine huts, hostels, cabins and motels throughout the park. Most day-use areas and trailheads are well signed from the highway and many are highlighted on park maps, websites and in visitor guides.

The hiking season can be very short in some places, especially at higher elevations. In some cases, trails may not be snow free until early to mid-July and can become snowbound by early October. Many viewpoints and attractions along the Icefields Parkway and near town are accessible year-round and are popular stops even in the winter months.

There are numerous waterfalls along both routes through Jasper National Park, many of them visible and accessible, while some, although impressive, have access to them obstructed by river crossings or bushwhacking. Driving distances to trailheads are given from either the Icefield information centre in the southern portion of the park or from the town of Jasper in the northern part.

While driving directions for each hike are provided using the town of Jasper as the starting point, the following waypoints are provided for each direction of travel on Highway 93:

Jasper	0 km	Trans-Canada Highway: Lake Louise	0 km
Wabasso Road: Athabasca Falls	32 km	Bow Lake	35 km
Sunwapta Falls	55 km	Saskatchewan Crossing	75 km
Sunwapta Station: Poboktan Creek	70 km	Columbia Icefields	125 km
Columbia Icefields	103 km	Sunwapta Station: Poboktan Creek	158 km
Saskatchewan Crossing	153 km	Sunwapta Falls	173 km
Bow Lake	193 km	Wabasso Road: Athabasca Falls	196 km
Trans-Canada Highway: Lake Louise	228 km	Jasper	228 km

For more information contact the Jasper National Park visitor centre:
pc.gc.ca/en/pn-np/ab/jasper
500 Connaught Drive, Jasper, AB T0E 1E0
(780) 852-6176
Camping reservations: 1-888-737-3783

TANGLE FALLS

1. Tangle Falls

LOCATION: Jasper National Park
DRIVING DIFFICULTY: Easy
HIKING DIFFICULTY: Easy
HIKING DISTANCE: Ask the chicken...
HIKING TIME: N/A

Q: Why did the chicken cross the road?
A: Because... Tangle Falls!

Tangle Falls is one of the more spectacular and recognizable waterfalls in Jasper National Park. Although the Icefields Parkway is peppered with jaw-dropping sights from one end to the other, Tangle Falls stands apart as a cascade you can get up close and personal with just by wandering across the road.

Driving directions

From the Columbia Icefield visitor centre, drive north on Highway 93 for 7 km to a pullout on the left-hand (east) side of the highway. This is signed as a viewpoint on approach, with a more ornate wooden sign designating the parking area for Tangle Creek. There are pit

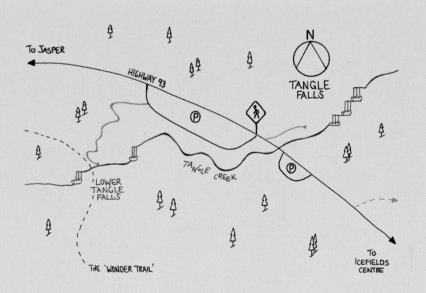

toilets and waste bins in the parking lot. The speed limit is reduced to 60 km/h along this stretch of road, as folks are frequently crossing and often walking on the highway itself to capture photos.

Hiking directions

Follow the chicken! Tangle Falls is directly across the highway from the parking area. It is possible to scramble up alongside the many tiers of Tangle Falls on both sides of the cataract. Take extra care if you choose to strut like a chicken across the road, though. The pull-out is along a curved section of the highway, and inattentive motorists may be caught off guard by the presence of pedestrians milling about on the thoroughfare.

It takes two to tangle

Long before a highway graced the floor of the Sunwapta and Athabasca river valleys, the historic travel route traversed over Wilcox Pass to avoid Sunwapta Canyon below Tangle Falls. These horseback excursions required a descent from the pass back down into the valley via Tangle Creek, and a tangle is exactly what they found: steep, dense forest with creeks and waterfalls... and no highway.

2. Lower Tangle Falls

LOCATION: Jasper National Park
DRIVING DIFFICULTY: Easy
HIKING DIFFICULTY: Easy
HIKING DISTANCE: 100 m
HIKING TIME: 2 min

While Tangle Falls is the obvious prize here, there are two cataracts below the highway on Tangle Creek that make up Lower Tangle Falls. Both are spectacular and beautiful in their own right and are hidden just enough to avoid detection by most people.

Driving directions

From the Columbia Icefield visitor centre, drive north on Highway 93 for 7 km to a pullout on the left-hand (east) side of the highway. This is signed as a viewpoint on approach, with a more ornate wooden sign designating the parking for Tangle Creek. There are pit toilets and waste bins in the parking area. The speed limit is reduced to 60 km/h along this stretch, as folks are frequently crossing (and often walking right on the highway itself) to capture photos.

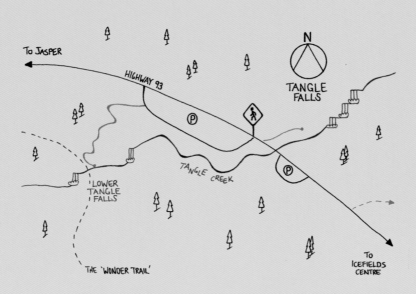

Hiking directions

Walk to the northernmost point of the northernmost parking area for Tangle Falls. Pick up a trail that descends briefly but steeply through the trees beside a waterfall. A chunk of the original Icefields Parkway can be seen below. Use caution scrambling down a rocky stretch to the road. From here you will be at the base of one waterfall and directly above another. It is not recommended to proceed beyond this point. A bridge that used to span Tangle Creek is slowly being reclaimed by nature, with rebar and other steel components exposed amid the deteriorating concrete.

The "Wonder Trail"

It is a great injustice to tell this story in a single paragraph. Before the bustling highway that is driven today, there was the original single-lane road on which you now stand. A snaking, 230-km gravel pathway connected

the villages of Lake Louise and Jasper. Construction began in 1931 and was completed about ten years later. Soon the rise in the availability and affordability of automobiles saw tourism explode in the parks. In 1962 the road was paved and realigned to accommodate the booming popularity of the drive. Portions of the original highway can be found throughout Banff and Jasper national parks, although the vegetation is slowly moving back in. The Wonder Trail was conceived by A.O. Wheeler, lead surveyor on the BC/Alberta Boundary Commission.

There are some excellent articles from Parks Canada and various other sources on the rich history of the Icefields Parkway.

3. Beauty Creek Waterfalls

LOCATION: Jasper National Park
DRIVING DIFFICULTY: Easy
HIKING DIFFICULTY: Easy
HIKING DISTANCE: 1.6 km
HIKING TIME: 30 min

Nowhere in the Rockies is the assignment of a name more fitting than here at Beauty Creek. And nowhere in the Rockies will you find a higher concentration of waterfalls in a single location. Don't take the nondescript nature of the highway pullout as an indication of what you will find here: waterfall after waterfall after glorious waterfall.

Driving directions

From the Columbia Icefield visitor centre, drive north on Highway 93 for 15.2 km to a small pullout on the right-hand side of the highway signed for Beauty Creek.

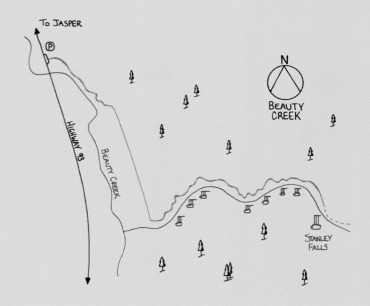

Hiking directions

From the parking area, follow a well-used pathway that wanders briefly through the trees until it meets a decommissioned roadway. Turn right and follow the road until it nears Beauty Creek. A trail leaves the road on the left (900 m from the trailhead) and begins a gradual ascent alongside Beauty Creek and its many waterfalls.

There are eight cataracts in total (including Stanley Falls, highlighted separately). It is about 30 minutes to Stanley Falls, although it is worth budgeting a little longer to rubberneck and snap photos along the way.

Hostels on the Parkway

An alternative to frontcountry camping or pricey overnight stays in hotels or lodges is a night in a hostel. Hostelling International operates ten such facilities in the Canadian Rockies, with several along the Icefields Parkway in Banff and Jasper national parks and one at Beauty Creek. These generally include shared dormitory-style rooms (although some do offer smaller private rooms). Many of these "wilderness hostels" do not have electricity or running water, but they are often equipped with fuel for lighting and cooking. For more information and reservations, visit **hihostels.ca**.

4. Stanley Falls

LOCATION: Jasper National Park
DRIVING DIFFICULTY: Easy
HIKING DIFFICULTY: Easy
HIKING DISTANCE: 1.6 km
HIKING TIME: 30 min

As you wander alongside the turquoise waters of Beauty Creek and pass by a series of stunning waterfalls, it is hard to imagine a better return on investment. In fact, other than an ill-fated Ponzi scheme, if any other proposition included a guaranteed 8:1 ROI, one would probably be inclined to alert the authorities. But even if you did want to do that, there's no cell service here anyway. Enjoy the hike!

Driving directions

From the Columbia Icefield visitor centre, drive north on Highway 93 for 15.2 km to a small pullout on the right-hand side of the highway.

Hiking directions

From the parking area, follow a well-used pathway that wanders briefly through the trees until it meets a decommissioned roadway. Turn right and follow the road until it nears Beauty Creek. A trail leaves the road on the left (900 m from the trailhead) and begins a gradual ascent alongside Beauty Creek and its many waterfalls, Stanley Falls being the largest and final one (1.6 km from the trailhead).
   See also Beauty Creek Waterfalls.

The Stanley Cup of waterfalls

Lord Stanley of Preston has lent his name to many places, buildings and establishments across this fine country. In addition to the spectacular Stanley Falls, his name also graces the National Hockey League's top prize, the infamous Stanley Park in Vancouver, Stanley Peak in Kootenay National Park and many streets in Canada and Australia. Frederick Stanley was the sixth Governor General of Canada, serving from 1888 to 1893.

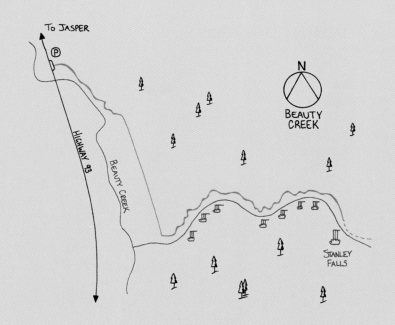

To JASPER

N

BEAUTY
CREEK

Highway 93

Beauty Creek

STANLEY
FALLS

5. Poboktan Falls

LOCATION: Jasper National Park
DRIVING DIFFICULTY: Easy
HIKING DIFFICULTY: Difficult (due to distance; overnight recommended)
HIKING DISTANCE: 12.0 km
HIKING TIME: 4–5 h

While Poboktan Creek doesn't offer the high-elevation vistas that many of the more popular hikes in Jasper National Park do, it serves as a mellow overnight stay in the backcountry and is the gateway to many other places such as Maligne, Poboktan and Jonas passes. Poboktan Falls is a little dash of added incentive along the way.

Driving directions

From the junction of Highways 93 and 16 near the town of Jasper, drive south on Highway 93 for 70.0 km. Cross the bridge over Poboktan Creek and turn left into a large parking area signed for Poboktan.

Hiking directions

The trail starts on the north side of the creek near the Sunwapta Station warden's cabin, but the large parking area is on the south side of the creek. From the parking lot, walk back to the highway, then north on the bridge over Poboktan Creek and onto the access roadway into the Parks compound. Head back towards the creek and locate a trailhead kiosk and signage for the trail.

Hike the Poboktan Creek trail for 6.4 km to a junction. Head right at the junction, following directions for the Waterfalls campground. Cross the bridge over the creek and continue for an additional 5.6 km. At 12.0 km Poboktan Falls comes into view alongside the trail. The falls are tall and wide, with numerous tiers and cascades.

The Waterfalls campground is just another hundred metres farther. Cross the bridge over a small stream, where a short uphill jaunt leads to the campground's cooking area overlooking the falls. The campsites are just a little farther.

6. Unnamed Falls (Contour Falls)

LOCATION: Jasper National Park
DRIVING DIFFICULTY: Easy
HIKING DIFFICULTY: Difficult (due to distance; overnight recommended)
HIKING DISTANCE: 12.3 km
HIKING TIME: 4–5 h

This is one of the most unique waterfalls in the Rockies, a sight which few are aware of and even fewer have ventured to. Water from high above on Poboktan Mountain rockets down a slender gash in an immense stone slab, making this waterfall distinct from nearly every other one in the book.

Driving directions

From the junction of Highways 93 and 16 near the town of Jasper, drive south on Highway 93 for 70.0 km. Cross the bridge over Poboktan Creek and turn left into a large parking area signed for Poboktan.

Hiking directions

The trail starts on the north side of the creek near the Sunwapta Station warden's cabin. From the parking area, walk back to the highway, then north on the bridge over Poboktan Creek and onto the access road for the Parks compound. Head back towards the creek and locate a trailhead kiosk and signage for the trail.

Hike the Poboktan Creek trail for 6.4 km to a junction. Head right at the junction, following directions for the Waterfalls campground. Cross the bridge over the creek and continue for an additional 5.6 km. At 12.0 km, near Poboktan Falls, cross a small stream on a wooden footbridge. The trail bends to the left and starts a brief ascent toward the campground. As the trail bends back to the right, pick up a faint trail that continues along the stream. The boot-beaten trail passes a series of smaller cascades before arriving at the base of the impressive waterfall pictured here.

7. Sunwapta Falls

LOCATION: Jasper National Park
DRIVING DIFFICULTY: Easy
HIKING DIFFICULTY: Easy
HIKING DISTANCE: <100 m (depending on how close you can park)
HIKING TIME: 1 min

Sunwapta Falls is one of the iconic scenes located along the Icefields Parkway, an impressive rock funnel channelling the Sunwapta River under the eyes of its adoring fans. The river is fed year-round by the equally iconic Athabasca Glacier at the Columbia Icefield to the south. It is one of the most popular stops along the highway, especially in the busy summer months. Unless you arrive early in the morning or later in the evening, expect to be jostling for the prime viewing spots with local and foreign tourists as well as shutter-happy social media enthusiasts.

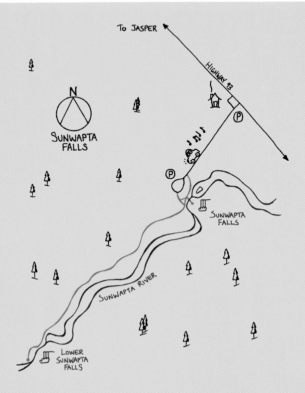

Driving directions

From the junction of Highways 93 and 16 near the town of Jasper, drive south on Highway 93 for 55 km to a turnoff signed for Sunwapta Falls Lodge. Turn right and follow the road to a parking area and turnaround at its end. There are outhouse facilities, picnic tables and garbage bins at the busy trailhead.

Hiking directions

Take a number and follow the crowd! The falls are easily accessible every day of the year and are a popular destination for tourists and local photographers alike.

What's in a name?

Sunwapta is a Stoney/Nakoda word for "turbulent water," gifted to the river by geologist and preeminent Rockies explorer Arthur (A.P.) Coleman. Many of the place names in Jasper National Park, and throughout much of Alberta for that matter, originate from Indigenous languages: *Poboktan, Yamnuska* and *Minnewanka* (Stoney/Nakoda for "owl," "wall of rock" and "water of the spirits," respectively); *Athabasca* and *Kananaskis* (Cree for "where there are reeds" and "meeting of the waters"); *Ponoka* and *Okotoks* (Blackfoot for "elk" and "big rock"), to name just a few.

PHOTO: BRIGID SCOTT

8. Lower Sunwapta Falls

LOCATION: Jasper National Park
DRIVING DIFFICULTY: Easy
HIKING DIFFICULTY: Easy
HIKING DISTANCE: 2.0 km
HIKING TIME: 30–45 min

Something to know about the national parks is that 95 per cent of the guests never stray more than a hundred metres from their vehicle. Also, 95 per cent of statistics are made up on the spot... so do with that information as you please. Most visitors to Sunwapta Falls are content to mill around the bridge and gush over the main falls. Few are even aware of this short and (relatively) quiet hike to the lower waterfall. The Sunwapta River continues downstream through a series of steps and small canyons to a second waterfall before its eventual confluence with the Athabasca River.

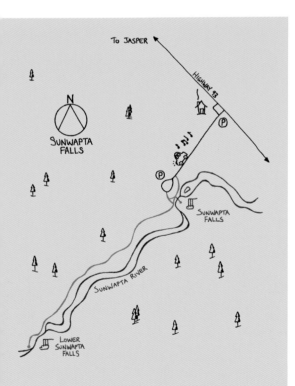

Driving directions

From the junction of Highways 93 and 16 near the town of Jasper, drive south on Highway 93 for 55 km to a signed junction at Sunwapta Falls Lodge. Turn right and follow the road to a parking area and turnaround at its end. There are outhouse facilities, picnic tables and garbage bins at the busy trailhead.

Hiking directions

From the parking area, follow trailhead signage for the lower falls trail. A well-trodden pathway descends gently through

the forest before reaching a series of fenced viewpoints above and below the lower falls.

The mighty Athabasca

From its icy source high on the expansive Columbia Icefield, the Athabasca River begins its 1231-kilometre journey to Lake Athabasca. From this point it becomes a tributary of the Mackenzie River en route to the Arctic Ocean. Alberta's longest river has an equally long history and has served to facilitate exploration and trade going back to the late 1700s. Today the Athabasca remains an important stream for biodiversity, but it is under constant pressure from human impacts including recreation, forestry, agriculture and resource development.

9. *Athabasca Falls*

LOCATION: Jasper National Park
DRIVING DIFFICULTY: Easy
HIKING DIFFICULTY: Easy
HIKING DISTANCE: negligible
HIKING TIME: subject to time needed to navigate crowds. If all goes well, also negligible

Similar to its comrade farther upstream, Athabasca Falls is close to the highway and only a short stroll from the parking area. For this reason, it commands the attention of thousands of people per day, marching single file to fulfill their mission of obtaining the same photo that the previous person captured. An acceptable, albeit jaded, alternative if time and patience run thin is to visit a gas station or gift shop and snap a photo of a postcard of Athabasca Falls. Follow me for more life hacks!

Driving directions

From the junction of Highways 93 and 16 near the town of Jasper, drive south on Highway 93 for 30 km to an intersection with Highway 93A – Wabasso Road and ample signage for Athabasca Falls. Turn right onto Highway 93A, and shortly after turn left into a large parking and picnic area.

Hiking directions

From the parking area, head towards the river and weave through throngs of tourists armed with selfie sticks and cameras. There are a number of places to

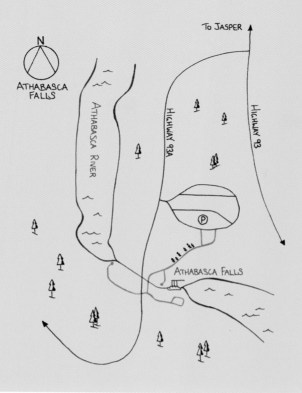

view the falls on both sides of the river as well as from a bridge just downstream of the falls.

The early birdy gets the wormy

Many of the major attractions in Jasper National Park get busy early in the day and stay full of activity well into the evening. If you intend to visit places like Athabasca Falls, Sunwapta Falls and Maligne Canyon, best to break camp early, get breakfast on the go and arrive before 9:00 a.m. Any later and you may find yourself relegated to parking on the shoulder of the highway. These hot spots stay busy long after dinner, but by 8:00 p.m. the crowds will start to thin and parking becomes available once again.

10. *Lower Geraldine Falls*

LOCATION: Jasper National Park
DRIVING DIFFICULTY: Moderate
HIKING DIFFICULTY: Easy
HIKING DISTANCE: 3.0 km
HIKING TIME: 1.5 h

Geraldine Lakes is a recognizable name to many, yet most visitors to the area are generally content to mill around the valley bottom. The steep fire road to the trailhead has proven to be an effective deterrent to keep would-be assailants at bay. The rewards along this trail for a little extra effort are plentiful, relative solitude being one of them. Lakes, mountain views and waterfalls round out the list nicely.

Driving directions

From the junction of Highways 93 and 16 near the town of Jasper, drive south on Highway 93 for 30 km. Turn right onto Highway 93A,

Wabasso Road and follow for 1 km to a pullout and staging area for Geraldine Lakes. Turn left and drive the steep, gravel road for 6 km to the Geraldine Lakes trailhead.

Hiking directions

From the parking area, start up a well-used trail into the trees. Although the path is criss-crossed with tree roots and occasionally muddy, the trail is well maintained to the first lake which is reached after 1.8 km. Once at the lake, continue on the trail around the lake in a counter-clockwise direction. The far end of the lake is reached in another 1 km. From this point, the trail is a bit indistinct through a rocky slope. The falls are a short distance farther.

11. Geraldine Falls

LOCATION: Jasper National Park
DRIVING DIFFICULTY: Moderate
HIKING DIFFICULTY: Moderate
HIKING DISTANCE: 4.5 km
HIKING TIME: 2 h

Geraldine Falls is a spectacular sight: a large waterfall crashing down a headwall flanked by tall mountains on either side. Without the benefit of a well-groomed trail and with access being via a steep gravel road, the tourist traffic is all but weeded out from this hike.

Driving directions

From the junction of Highways 93 and 16 near the town of Jasper, drive south on Highway 93 for 30 km. Turn right onto Highway 93A, Wabasso Road, and follow for 1 km to a pullout and staging area for Geraldine Lakes. Turn left and drive the steep gravel road for 6 km to the Geraldine Lakes trailhead.

Hiking directions

From the parking area, start up a well-used trail into the trees. Although the path is criss-crossed with tree roots and occasionally muddy, the trail is well maintained to the first lake, which is reached after 1.8 km. Once at the lake, continue on the trail around the lake in a counter-clockwise direction. The far end of the lake is reached in another 1 km, with the lower falls a short distance farther – 3.0 km to this point.

From the lower falls the trail climbs steeply for a couple hundred metres before levelling out in a boulder field. At this point the trail becomes indistinct, but cairns mark the way for the next 300 m as you hop from rock to rock with the impressive Geraldine Falls becoming visible on the horizon. Reach a small tarn at 3.5 km, at which point the trail becomes much more defined again and travels clockwise around the tarn. Reach the base of Geraldine Falls at 4.5 km.

Important to note that this hike is NOT recommended if it has been raining or if there is rain in the forecast. The roots on the lower portion of the trail and the lichen on the boulders become extremely slippery and dangerous.

To HIGHWAY 93A
& JASPER

GERALDINE ROAD

FIRST
GERALDINE
LAKE

LOWER
GERALDINE
FALLS

N

GERALDINE
LAKES

GERALDINE
FALLS

SECOND
GERALDINE
LAKE

More to explore: Second Geraldine Lake

Above Geraldine Falls the trail ascends a steep head-wall en route to the second Geraldine Lake. There is a backcountry campground at the far end of the second lake. It is 6.2 km to the campground, with over 600 metres of elevation gain. The trip can be extended farther to two other lakes via a crude alpine route.

12. *Angel Glacier Falls*

LOCATION: Jasper National Park
DRIVING DIFFICULTY: Easy
HIKING DIFFICULTY: Easy
HIKING DISTANCE: 1 km
HIKING TIME: 15 min

In the shadow of Mount Edith Cavell, the waterfall draining Angel Glacier is a spectacular sight and one of Jasper's primo postcard-worthy views. These are the types of vistas that epitomize Canada's national parks network and draw people from all around the world.

Driving directions

From the town of Jasper, drive south on Highway 93 for 7 km and turn right onto Highway 93A – Wabasso Road (signed). Follow Highway 93A for 5.4 km and turn right onto Cavell Road (also signed). Follow the narrow, winding and recently paved road for 14 km to its end in a large parking area (signed yet again).

Important to note that trailers and motorhomes are not permitted to use this road. Trailers can be unhitched and left in a designated trailer parking area off Highway 93. The road is open from June 20 to October 15 seasonally, subject to snowfall.

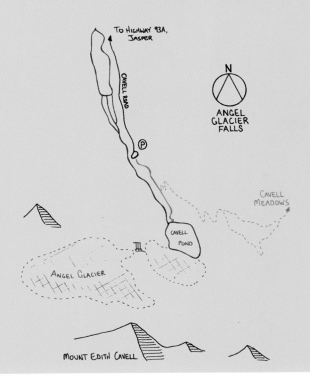

Hiking directions

From the parking area, walk up the stone stairs and follow a paved trail to a viewpoint under the immense north face of Mount Edith Cavell. Clinging to the dark wall high above the trail is the spectacular Angel Glacier and a beautiful cascade of icy water tumbling towards Cavell Pond below.

More to explore: Cavell Meadows

High above the paved Path of the Glacier trail is one of the most sought-after day hikes in the Canadian Rockies: Cavell Meadows. The 3 km trail climbs steadily to a fragile alpine environment high above the crowds, with increasingly amazing views of the world below. The season to explore the high alpine trail is short, typically mid-July through the end of the summer, to protect the delicate environment. Check trail conditions and closures by visiting the Parks Canada website and time your visit accordingly.

13. Maligne Canyon

LOCATION: Jasper National Park
DRIVING DIFFICULTY: Easy
HIKING DIFFICULTY: Easy
HIKING DISTANCE: 3.7 km
HIKING TIME: 1.5 h

Maligne Canyon is Jasper National Park's answer to Johnston Canyon near Banff. Don't let the crowds deter you, though. Wake the kids up early, feast on granola bars in the car and arrive before 9:00 a.m. so you can explore the canyon with relatively little traffic. Here, the waters of the Maligne River are squeezed into a deep, narrow gorge which hikers can observe from high above via a network of pathways and a series of bridges. This is world-class scenery for a reason and not to be missed! For a unique family photo, leave the pyjamas on; it will also save you seven to ten minutes on your departure.

Driving directions

From the junction of Highways 93 and 16 near Jasper, drive east on Highway 16 for 3 km to Maligne Road (signed). Turn right, cross the Athabasca River, then stay left for Maligne Canyon and Maligne Lake. The main parking area is 6.1 km up this road and located at the top of the canyon.

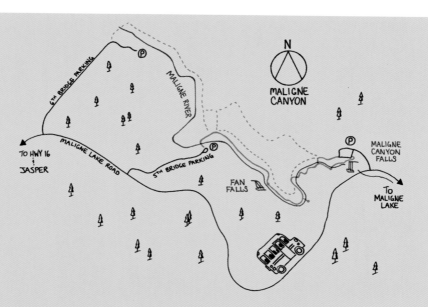

There are also parking areas for Sixth Bridge at 2 km and Fifth Bridge at 3 km, which are signed along Maligne Road.

Hiking directions

Hiking directions are given from the main parking areas, from First Bridge to Sixth Bridge. From parking, walk east past the café towards the river, then stay right following alongside the river before it drops into the canyon. Maligne Canyon Falls are visible from First Bridge, 200 m from the parking area. Personally, I recommend the hike from Sixth Bridge to the top and return via the loop trail.

- From First Bridge, continue downstream for 200 m to Second Bridge. This is one of the deepest parts of the canyon, at over 50 m.

- From Second Bridge, continue downstream for 250 m to Third Bridge. There is another waterfall at this point, commonly called Double Falls.

- From Third Bridge, continue downstream for 300 m to Fourth Bridge. Here the river exits the canyon.

- From Fourth Bridge, continue downstream for 1.2 km to Fifth Bridge, passing Fan Falls and several springs along the way.

- From Fifth Bridge, continue downstream for 1.6 km to Sixth Bridge. This portion of the hike is in the forest along the Maligne River.

14. Fan Falls

LOCATION: Jasper National Park
DRIVING DIFFICULTY: Easy
HIKING DIFFICULTY: Easy
HIKING DISTANCE: 1.4 km
HIKING TIME: 30 min

Fan Falls is along the Maligne Canyon trail and is generally seen as part of a loop from the main parking area. But it also makes a great stand-alone short hike from the Fifth Bridge and is on a portion of the trail network that sees far less traffic. This delicate cascade is a groundwater spring, one of several that feed the Maligne River near the outlet of the canyon.

Driving directions

From the junction of Highways 93 and 16 near Jasper, drive east on Highway 16 for 3 km to Maligne Road (signed). Turn right, cross the Athabasca River, then stay left for Maligne Canyon and Maligne Lake. Drive Maligne Road for 2.9 km, then turn left onto a road signed for Fifth Bridge. The parking area is a short way down this road.

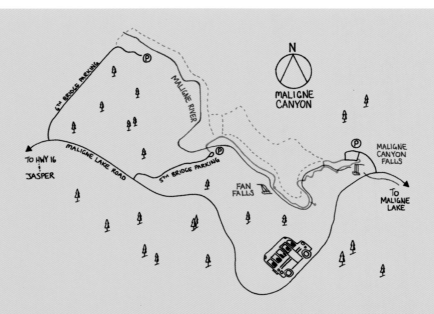

Hiking directions

From the parking area, cross the recently constructed Fifth Bridge, then stay right, following signs for First Bridge. The trail ascends briefly and cuts across an open slope before dropping back down to the river across from Fan Falls. From here you can return the way you came or continue up the Maligne Canyon trail network.

15. Punchbowl Falls

LOCATION: Jasper National Park
DRIVING DIFFICULTY: Easy
HIKING DIFFICULTY: Easy
HIKING DISTANCE: A few metres
HIKING TIME: A few seconds

Punchbowl Falls is an attractive cataract that makes for a quick stop for those heading for a soak at Miette Hot Springs or a quick stretch of the legs for those travelling to and from Jasper.

Driving directions

From the junction of Highways 93 and 16 near Jasper, drive east on Highway 16 for 45 km to Miette Road (signed). Turn right and follow Miette Road for 1.2 km to a large pullout on the right. The pullout is unsigned, but a small trailhead sign in the parking area denotes Punchbowl Falls.

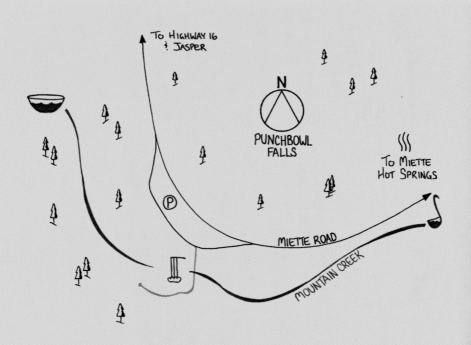

Hiking directions

From the parking area, a trail immediately crosses over Mountain Creek, directly above Punchbowl Falls. The view looking down from the bridge is very cool, the waterfall slipping down a narrow, polished chasm. Continue along the trail for a few metres to a lookout protected with fencing. From here the view of the falls is mostly obscured.

More to explore: Miette Hot Springs

Leave your hiking shoes for this one. All you need is your bathing suit and towel for the short stroll from the parking lot to the popular Miette Hot Springs. The hot pools are a bustling venue, even during the warm summer months. They are least busy first thing in the morning, although they will probably feel a whole lot better to you after you've tackled the Sulphur Skyline hike or a scramble up Utopia Mountain.

16. Conifer Creek Waterfalls

LOCATION: Jasper National Park
DRIVING DIFFICULTY: Easy
HIKING DIFFICULTY: Easy
HIKING DISTANCE: 100 m
HIKING TIME: 5 min

Conifer Creek is a legitimate hidden gem off Highway 16, with its two-tiered waterfall completely obscured from the road. Only the keenest of rubbernecking navigators will notice the turbulent water through the cloak of trees and even fewer will make the effort to stop.

Driving directions

From the junction of Highways 93 and 16 near Jasper, drive west on Highway 16 for 7.7 km. There is a very small, unsigned pullout on the left (south) side of the highway. Take extra care entering and exiting the pullout, as visibility is somewhat restricted for oncoming traffic.

Hiking directions

From the pullout, a faint trail enters the trees beside the creek. Once you are into this forest, the lower waterfall presents itself. Continue scrambling up the slope on the right side of the creek to the base of the second waterfall.

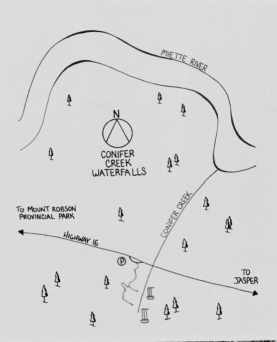

MIETTE RIVER

N

CONIFER
CREEK
WATERFALLS

TO MOUNT ROBSON
PROVINCIAL PARK

HIGHWAY 16

CONIFER CREEK

P

TO
JASPER

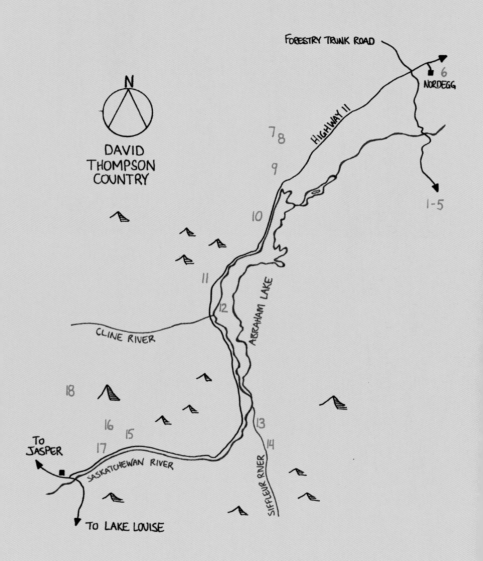

N

DAVID
THOMPSON
COUNTRY

FORESTRY TRUNK ROAD

NORDEGG
6

HIGHWAY 11

7 8

9

1-5

10

CLINE RIVER

11

12

ABRAHAM LAKE

13

14

18

16

15

17

To
JASPER

SASKATCHEWAN RIVER

SIFFLEUR RIVER

TO LAKE LOUISE

David Thompson Country and the Front Ranges

While many hikers, tourists and locals flock to the well-signed trailheads of the national and provincial parks, Alberta's front ranges and David Thompson Country offer a slightly different experience: unsigned trails, unsigned trailheads, unsigned roads and even unsigned signs. Throughout the dark ages, before smartphones, GPS devices and trail apps, people felt their way around this part of the world almost by Braille. It would not be unusual to see the same vehicle full of screaming kids pass back and forth near their destination multiple times before ultimately giving up or desperately flagging down another passerby. Even in our technologically superior era, some head-scratching remains when it comes to this corner of the province.

Although cellular service is sparse in these areas, you can take comfort knowing that we have already driven past all these trails multiple times in an effort to provide the most accurate information possible. This chapter covers the Highway 11 corridor from Saskatchewan Crossing to Nordegg, as well as a few hidden (and not so hidden) gems scattered throughout Alberta's foothills and front ranges.

While driving directions for each hike generally use Nordegg as the starting point, the following waypoints are provided for each direction of travel on Highway 11:

Saskatchewan Crossing	0 km	Nordegg	0 km
Owen Creek Trailhead	6.0 km	Jct Hwy 734 (Forestry Trunk Rd)	2.2 km
Thompson Creek Rec Site	9.5 km	Crescent Falls Rec Site	18.0 km
Siffleur Falls Trailhead	28.0 km	Tershishner Creek Trail	26.0 km
David Thompson Resort	44.0 km	Allstones Creek Rec Site	31.5 km
Whitegoat Falls Trailhead	47.0 km	Whitegoat Falls Trailhead	43.0 km
Allstones Creek Rec Site	58.5 km	David Thompson Resort	46.0 km
Tershishner Creek Trail	64.0 km	Siffleur Falls Trailhead	62.0 km
Crescent Falls Rec Site	72.0 km	Thompson Creek Rec Site	81.5 km
Jct Hwy 734 (Forestry Trunk Rd)	87.8 km	Owen Creek Trailhead	84.0 km
Nordegg	90.0 km	Saskatchewan Crossing	90.0 km

Many recreation sites, parking areas and trails are user-maintained. As with all outdoor pursuits, always pack out what you pack in, practise the Leave No Trace principles and leave the trailheads, trails and campsites in better shape than you found them. David Thompson Country is a spectacular wilderness environment, but much of it is without the benefit of protection by the provincial or national park system.

1. *Bighorn Falls*

LOCATION: Ya Ha Tinda Ranch, AB
DRIVING DIFFICULTY: Moderate
HIKING DIFFICULTY: Easy
HIKING DISTANCE: 400 m
HIKING TIME: 10 min

Ya Ha Tinda Ranch is a grassy oasis tucked into the eastern slopes of the Canadian Rockies. The historic spread is managed by Parks Canada and serves as the training ground for horses being groomed for patrolling western Canada's national parks. The grasslands act as a prime salad bar not only for the horses but also for elk wintering in the area. With relatively little vehicle traffic, wildlife is in great abundance in this montane region of the eastern slopes of the Rockies' front ranges.

Driving directions

From the junction of Highway 1A and Hwy 40 (Forestry Trunk Road) near the Ghost Lake reservoir, drive north on Highway 40 for 82 km

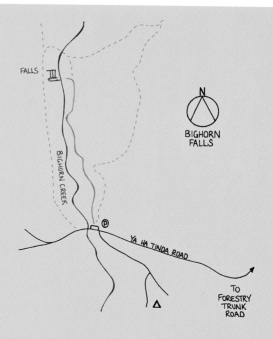

and cross over the Red Deer River to a prominent junction (the road is paved for the first 27.5 km and then becomes a well-maintained gravel surface). At the junction, turn left, following signs for Ya Ha Tinda Ranch. From the junction, drive on good gravel for 22.5 km to the Bighorn day-use area at Ya Ha Tinda. Park in a small gravel parking lot on the right with a trailhead and information kiosk.

Hiking directions

From the parking area, follow a wide pathway up a hill as it ascends briefly beside Bighorn Creek. The trail levels off within a few minutes and shortly after that you'll find yourself at the first of two viewpoints looking out over the impressive Bighorn Falls.

The montane ecoregion

The montane zone is an ecosystem that occurs within an elevation range below the subalpine and is characterized by its grasslands and mixed forests. This ecosystem is typically warmer and drier, especially in the winter months, making it attractive to both wildlife and humans. It is here in the montane biome that the greatest biodiversity in the Rockies can be observed in both wildlife and vegetation.

2. James Falls

LOCATION: Ya Ha Tinda Ranch, AB
DRIVING DIFFICULTY: Moderate
HIKING DIFFICULTY: Easy
HIKING DISTANCE: 4.8 km
HIKING TIME: 2 h

While Bighorn Falls is the main attraction for visitors to Ya Ha Tinda Ranch, that stroll is sufficiently short to allow for a second hike to James Falls. The waterfall is a narrow cascade tucked into the southern flanks of Eagle Mountain and located between Eagle Lake and James Lake.

Driving directions

From the junction of Highway 1A and Hwy 40 (Forestry Trunk Road) near the Ghost Lake reservoir, drive north on Highway 40 for 82 km and cross over the Red Deer River to a prominent junction (the road is paved for the first 27.5 km and then becomes a well-maintained gravel surface). At the junction, turn left, following signs for Ya Ha Tinda. From the junction, continue on good gravel for 19.1 km to the

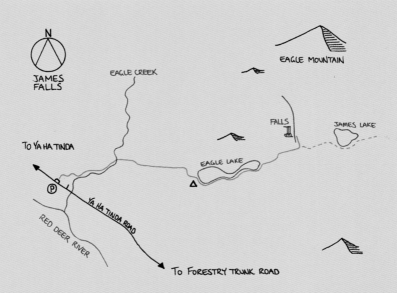

Eagle Lake day-use area. Park on the right in a large lot with trailhead signage and an information kiosk.

Hiking directions

From parking, follow the wide horse trail to Eagle Lake, 2.6 km from the trailhead. Continue past Eagle Lake, following the shoreline in a counter-clockwise direction. Past the lake and shortly after a small marshy area on the right, a gravel washout crosses the trail at 4.6 km. Locate a well-used trail, marked with a cairn, heading left up the rocky washout towards the base of Eagle Mountain. The falls can be heard from this point, which is an additional 200 m from the main trail.

The upper tier of the waterfall can also be accessed via a short scramble up steep slopes to the right of James Falls.

Note: The trail to Eagle Lake is mixed-use and frequented by folks on horseback. Keep your eyes and ears open and give the right of way to riders. Also, if there is any question which activity causes more trail destruction: horses, hikers, ATVs or dirtbikes, look no further than the puréed equestrian trail to Eagle Lake. At one point crossing a meadow there are 17 (yes, 17) trails side by side, a width that would be enviable to many motorists on a two-lane highway. Additionally, due to the heavy presence of four-legged animals and the obvious abundance of their waste, it is not advisable to fill your water bottle at Eagle Lake, Eagle Creek or the base of James Falls.

3. Table Rock and Tapestry Falls

LOCATION: Forestry Trunk Road, AB
DRIVING DIFFICULTY: Moderate
HIKING DIFFICULTY: Moderate
HIKING DISTANCE: 8.5 km
HIKING TIME: 3 h

At some point in any guidebook the author will have an internal struggle over whether to include an objective based on its worthiness or simply for filler. This hike is the latter. Would I take my kids here? No, they'd hate me. Would I take my wife here? Also no, I'd be signing divorce papers the next day. You may be asking yourself: *Steve, why, then, would you include this hike?*

Well, there is not one, not two, but three spectacular waterfalls. Sound enticing? It comes at a price. After two to three hours of weaving through old logging cutblocks and on skid roads that Mother Nature is quickly seeking to reclaim, the loooooong-awaited views of the Ram River and these waterfalls finally present themselves. The added bonus here is that you will, in all likelihood, "enjoy" the hiking in complete and utter solitude.

Driving directions

From the junction of Highway 11 and Hwy 734 (Forestry Trunk Road) near Nordegg, drive south on Hwy 734 for 72.5 km to an unmarked road on the left. Turn left and follow this road for 5.5 km. Turn right (small yellow sign for 5 km) and drive an additional 700 m to where the road is no longer drivable with a car – it's OHVs only beyond this point.

Hiking directions

From the end of the drivable road, you will connect a series of ATV trails followed by overgrown logging and skid roads. It is recommended to have a glance at a satellite image of the area and then preprogram the route into a GPS device or a mapping application on your smartphone. The logging roads are fast becoming overgrown and are often indistinct. If all else fails, head north. Directions and waypoints are as follows.

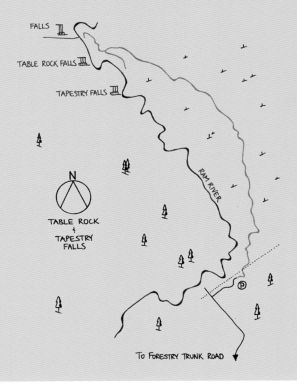

- 0.0 km – Start of ATV trail

- 0.15 km – Cross small stream, then stay left on another ATV trail

- 0.3 km – Stay right as another ATV trail joins from the left

- 0.5 km – Turn left onto another ATV trail. The trail is obvious for the next 2 km as it gently ascends through a wide forestry cut. Around 2.5 km the trail becomes indistinct at times; this is where having a satellite image of the logging roads will help.

- 7.0 km – The logging road descends towards the trees and ends near the edge of a mature forest. Flagging marks an obvious trail descending into the trees. It will reconnect with an ATV trail shortly after.

- 7.3 km – Primitive campsite in the trees, with boot-beaten trails going off in all directions. From here you can head to either Table Rock (lower) or Tapestry (upper) falls.

Table Rock Falls

From the campsite in the woods, descend slightly and follow a trail along the rim of the canyon, trending right (west). After about 800 m, the trail starts to descend towards the river and cuts across a steep dirt and scree slope. When you enter the trees again, descend a little farther before cutting left until the falls are in sight. Dropping all the way down to the river is less than safe and not advised. Return the way you came, 8.5 km from where you left your vehicle.

Tapestry Falls

From the campsite in the woods, cross a small stream and head back to the south. A faint trail on the canyon rim will lead to views of Tapestry Falls about 200 m farther. Descending into the canyon is similarly less than safe and not advised. Return the way you came, 7.7 km from where you left your vehicle.

Unnamed Falls

As a bonus for all your hard work, there is a beautiful three-tiered waterfall just north of Table Rock Falls where a small creek tumbles down through dark canyon walls to the Ram River below. It can be seen from the vantage point for Table Rock.

4. Ram Falls

LOCATION: Ram Falls Provincial Park, AB
DRIVING DIFFICULTY: Moderate
HIKING DIFFICULTY: Easy
HIKING DISTANCE: 400 m
HIKING TIME: 5-ish min

The long gravel road into Ram Falls deters few from visiting. After hours winding along the Forestry Trunk Road in the Rockies' front ranges, other vehicles become a strange sight. Yet, many make the dusty pilgrimage to take in the views of one of Alberta's finest landscapes. The clean, blue waters of the Ram River drop in impressive contrast to the dark walls of the surrounding canyon. Make sure your gas tank is full, the car is stocked with ample snacks and drinks, and all batteries are fully charged before setting out... it's a long way back to civilization.

Driving directions

From the junction of Highway 11 and Hwy 734 (Forestry Trunk Road) near Nordegg, drive south on Hwy 734 for 58.5 km to Ram Falls Provincial Park. Turn left into the campground and day-use area. Follow the road for 500 m to the Ram Falls viewpoint parking area.

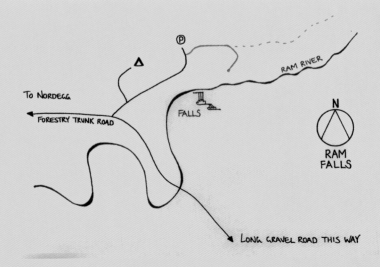

Hiking directions

Follow wide pathways for 300 m to the top of a large wooden staircase. Descend the stairs to a viewing platform perched on a slope above the Ram River and a front-row view of one of Alberta's most picturesque waterfalls.

The Forestry Trunk Road

Stretching roughly a thousand kilometres from Crowsnest Pass in southern Alberta to Grande Prairie in the north, the Forestry Trunk Road has long served as a critical link for industrial and recreational traffic alike. More than 800 km of the roadway is gravel, with the remaining 200 km being paved for better access to towns and provincial parks. It is labelled as Highway 40 and Hwy 734 along its length and can be accessed from numerous townships in Alberta's foothills.

When driving on the trunk road it is important to keep tabs on both your location and your gas tank. There are long stretches between gas stations and much of the road is without cell service. The trip from the Ghost Lake reservoir to Nordegg is 275 km, with more than 250 km of that being gravel. The road is generally well maintained and nicely graded, but dusty conditions should be expected, as well as much slower travel than on paved highways.

5. Hummingbird Creek Falls

LOCATION: Ram Falls Provincial Park, AB
DRIVING DIFFICULTY: Moderate
HIKING DIFFICULTY: Easy
HIKING DISTANCE: 200 m
HIKING TIME: 5 min

The remote Hummingbird Creek is a surprisingly popular spot for camping, fishing and hunting and makes for a great day out when combined with Ram Falls. Both hikes are short enough that they can easily be managed in a single trip in spite of the long drive.

Driving directions

From the junction of Highway 11 and Hwy 734 (Forestry Trunk Road) near Nordegg, drive south on Hwy 734 for 56 km to the junction with Hummingbird Road (signed). Turn right and follow for 7.3 km to pullouts on the right-hand side of the road. Alternatively, there is some space to park in the campground just a couple hundred metres farther.

Hiking directions

All trails lead to the creek! From the pullouts along Hummingbird Road, cross the gravel road and locate one of many paths that will quickly deliver you to Hummingbird Creek.

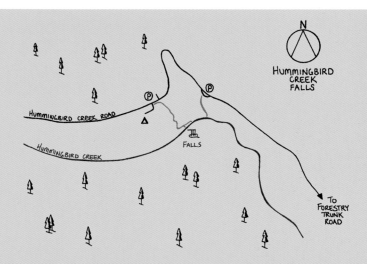

6. East Bush Falls

LOCATION: Nordegg, AB
DRIVING DIFFICULTY: Easy
HIKING DIFFICULTY: Easy
HIKING DISTANCE: 2.0 km
HIKING TIME: 40 min

The hike to East Bush Falls is a casual stroll on a mixed-use trail right in the small town of Nordegg. It is not unusual to come across ATVs on the trail network here. Keep your eyes and ears peeled and move well off to the side of the trail if you hear motorized users heading your way.

Driving directions

From the junction of Highway 11 and Stuart Street near Nordegg, drive south on Stuart to the Nordegg Heritage Centre and Museum on the right. Park in the visitor parking area.

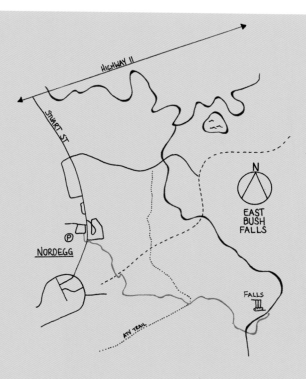

Hiking directions

From the museum parking lot, cross Stuart Street and continue south. Pick up an ATV trail that ascends a slope into the trees alongside an old graveyard. Directions from here are as follows:

- 0.5 km – Walk under an old wooden trestle then ascend a short steep trail on the left. Then stay right on the main ATV trail

- 0.7 km – Stay left (signed for East Bush Trail and Rail Trail)

- 1.2 km – Stay left (signed for East Bush Trail and Rail Trail)

- 1.4 km – Continue straight (signed for East Bush Trail)

- 1.7 km – Stay left (red arrow in trees)

- 1.8 km – Stream crossing

- 2.0 km – Top of waterfall. Continue down to the right on dirt trails to access the base of the falls

A brief history of Nordegg

Nordegg exists due primarily to coal mining in the early 1900s. At the request of the original stakeholder, Martin Nordegg (né Martin Cohn), Brazeau Collieries Ltd. was established to extract the coal. The Canadian Northern Railway arrived not long after and with it a camp. The town of Nordegg was formally founded in 1914. The mine was productive for nearly five decades but was not without its challenges. Between two world wars, a deadly explosion in 1941 and a fire in 1950, it was eventually financial troubles that saw the mine close in 1955 and many of the residents move away.

7. Unnamed Falls (Wapiabi Creek Falls)

LOCATION: Nordegg, AB
DRIVING DIFFICULTY: Moderate
HIKING DIFFICULTY: Easy
HIKING DISTANCE: 1.6 km
HIKING TIME: 40 min

When you arrive at the Crescent Falls day-use area, make a beeline for the two waterfalls on Wapiabi Creek first. While it may result in some raised eyebrows and confusion from the throngs of visitors heading to Crescent Falls, it will ensure that you've saved the best for last. These secluded waterfalls are very beautiful and very peaceful, but they pale in comparison to the big one near the parking area. The Wapiabi Falls are also known locally as Isaac's Falls and are a popular ice climb in the winter months, the name of the ice climb going by a slightly less appropriate moniker.

Driving directions

From the junction of Highway 11 and Stuart Street near Nordegg, drive west on Highway 11 for 18 km to a turnoff signed for the Crescent Falls recreation area. Turn right and follow a well-maintained gravel road for 6 km to a parking lot at the day-use area for Crescent Falls.

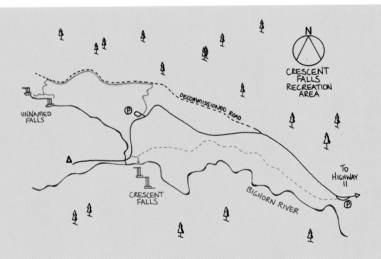

Hiking directions

From the parking area, an ATV trail signed for Wapiabi–Bighorn Ice Climb is located to the right of the outhouse. Follow this narrow dirt road for a couple hundred metres as it ascends through the trees until it intersects with another gravel road. Turn left (signed for Ice Climb) and follow for an additional 1.1 km (1.4 km from parking). A small, boot-beaten trail leaves the gravel road on the left (flagging in trees and small pile of rocks on road). The narrow trail descends gently for 200 m to a point above Wapiabi Falls.

To view the main (lower) waterfall, go left along the edge of a deep canyon until the falls are in view. As a waterfall, it is most impressive in late spring when the water in the creek is higher. Later in the summer it slows to little more than a trickle. In the winter the falls freeze up, forming a vertical wall of ice.

Bonus waterfall (Unnamed Falls – Upper Wapiabi Creek Falls)

There is a second, smaller waterfall just upstream from Wapiabi Creek Falls, only 150 metres away. From above the main falls, a faint trail leads off to the west through the forest. This small two-tiered waterfall will be visible within minutes, although you'll likely hear it before you see it. It is a great place to escape the crowd at the Crescent Falls viewpoint as well as the heat during the summer months.

8. *Crescent Falls*

LOCATION: Nordegg, AB
DRIVING DIFFICULTY: Moderate
HIKING DIFFICULTY: Easy
HIKING DISTANCE: 300 m to 2.5 km
HIKING TIME: 5 min to 1 h

Crescent Falls is by far one of the most picturesque and recognizable cascades in the province. Its two large cataracts are flanked by tall cliffs and are instantly recognizable. It's an iconic Alberta scene that simply has to be seen in person to realize that all the stunning images of this special place are actually not photoshopped after all.

Driving directions

From the junction of Highway 11 and Stuart Street near Nordegg, drive west on Highway 11 for 18 km to a turnoff signed for the Crescent Falls recreation area. Turn right and follow a well-maintained gravel road for 6 km to a parking lot at the day-use area for Crescent Falls.

Please note that the lower parking lot near the viewing area is reserved for accessible parking only.

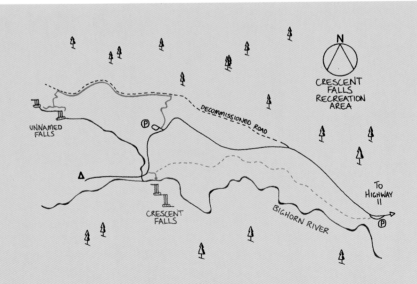

Hiking directions

From the day-use area, continue down the road for 300 m to the viewing platform next to the lower parking lot.

For an extended outing, you can hike the 2.5 km trail along the canyon rim high above the Bighorn River back towards the Bighorn Canyon Overlook (this is first parking lot on the drive in). The hike features fantastic views of the deep gorge as well as the falls from a distance.

In 2021 Alberta Parks erected barriers along the pathway rim to prevent visitors from descending very steep slopes to the base of the falls. These off-piste pathways were becoming excessively eroded, damaging vegetation, and had become unsafe.

Know before you go

Even though they are outside the national parks and feel a little bit more remote, Crescent Falls is a popular stop for visitors year-round. During the summer months, and especially on weekends, parking can back up for hundreds of metres along the narrow gravel access road. If visiting during the peak season, it is best to come early in the morning or later in the evening to secure both prime parking and prime viewing.

9. Tershishner Falls

LOCATION: Abraham Lake, AB
DRIVING DIFFICULTY: Easy
HIKING DIFFICULTY: Easy
HIKING DISTANCE: 1.7 km
HIKING TIME: 45 min

Tershishner Falls is a small waterfall and pales in comparison to nearby Crescent Falls. However, the lack of a signed trailhead or a marked and maintained trail means that it flies under the radar of many explorers. It also means that, unlike Crescent Falls, you won't have to jockey for position to view this one.

Driving directions

From the junction of Highway 11 and Stuart Street near Nordegg, drive west on Highway 11 for 26 km to an unsigned junction just west of the Tershishner Creek bridge. Turn right off the highway and immediately park off to the side of the gravel road.

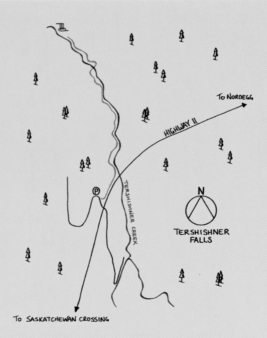

Hiking directions

From the parking area, walk back towards the highway and follow an ATV road in the ditch, heading east towards Tershishner Creek. As you approach the creek, stay left, following the ATV road. The trail follows the left-hand side of the creek, initially on the old road, although it is interrupted at a few spots due to washouts.

After 1.5 km, cross the creek via a large log. Once across, continue for an additional 200 m to the base of a small waterfall in a narrow canyon.

Flooding events have altered the trail somewhat in recent years, but it is well-flagged and easy to locate, even in the rocky creekbed.

Tershishner is a Stoney word for "burnt timber."

10. Allstones Falls

LOCATION: Abraham Lake, AB
DRIVING DIFFICULTY: Easy
HIKING DIFFICULTY: Difficult (due to creek crossings and travel in creek)
HIKING DISTANCE: 1.5 km
HIKING TIME: 1 h

Disclaimer: It is with some reluctance that this hike is included. There is a limited window in early summer where this route can be attempted safely. That is during a period where runoff has substantially ended but before the Abraham Lake reservoir is refilled. The hike involves numerous creek crossings which can be unsafe during periods of high streamflow.

Driving directions

From the junction of Highway 11 and Stuart Street near Nordegg, drive west on Highway 11 for 31.5 km to a day-use and camping area on the left signed for Allstones Creek. The day-use parking area is just before the causeway over the creek to the north, and the camping area is on the south side.

Hiking directions

From the parking area, cross Highway 11 and walk south along the road for 100 m to the south side of the creek. Descend to the creek and walk directly up the canyon for 1.5 km to the falls. Depending on streamflow, you may find yourself wading through the creek. A solid pair of sandals or water shoes is strongly recommended; expect to get your feet wet. Anticipate no less than twenty crossings of Allstones Creek.

Timing a visit to Allstones Falls can be tricky. If you arrive near the peak of runoff or after a heavy rain, the creek may be flowing high and fast enough to bar access to the canyon altogether or at least make the creek crossings difficult. If you come later in the summer when the Bighorn dam's outflow is reduced and Abraham Lake approaches full-pool, the water level comes up and actually floods the access to the canyon. You may need more than one attempt to check this one off your list; I needed three.

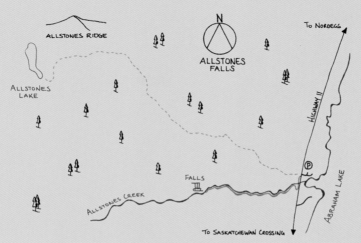

More to explore: Allstones Lake and Allstones Ridge

From the same parking area, cross the highway directly to a well-used trail with signage for Allstones Lake. It is 4 km one way to the lake on a steep trail that gains over 600 metres of elevation. From the lake, it is possible to continue up to a minor summit on Allstones Ridge.

11. *Whitegoat Falls*

LOCATION: Abraham Lake, AB
DRIVING DIFFICULTY: Easy
HIKING DIFFICULTY: Easy
HIKING DISTANCE: 1.5 km
HIKING TIME: 40 min

The two-tiered Whitegoat Falls is a spectacular small cascade that starts at yet another seemingly random trailhead. It's these small treasures that make the mountains worth exploring. Sure, the big vistas and trophy shots are what everyone wants to remember, but often when folks recall their adventures, it's the random encounters that tend to be the most memorable.

Driving directions

From the junction of Highway 11 and Stuart Street near Nordegg, drive west on Highway 11 for 43 km to a junction on the right signed for the Cline Waste Transfer Station. Follow a somewhat rough gravel road for just 200 m to a fenced yard. Parking is on the left, outside the fence.

Hiking directions

From the parking area, walk clockwise around the fenced enclosure and then turn left onto a gravel ATV trail. Follow the ATV track for 900 m as it climbs gently through a heavily forested area. On the left will be a well-used hiking trail signed for White Goat Falls. After 1.2 km the trail meets the rim of a shallow canyon. From here you have two options:

1. Descend from this point on a short, steep slope to the creek. Cross the creek on logs and follow the left-hand side of the creek for 200 m to another log crossing at the base of the falls. Note that this option may not be possible during runoff or after heavy rains or other periods of high stream flow.
2. Follow a high trail on the rim above the canyon for a couple hundred metres and then descend sharply, directly to the base of the falls. This slope is very steep and slick. Parents may have difficulty giving their children the hand they will likely need, as the grownups will be preoccupied with their own self-preservation.

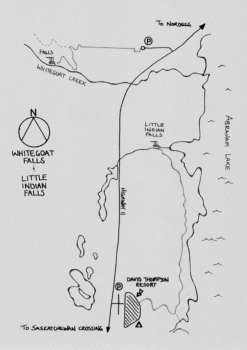

WHITEGOAT
FALLS
⁝
LITTLE
INDIAN
FALLS

Canyoning in the Canadian Rockies

These limestone giants are laced with narrow slots and canyons. Millions of years of snow, ice, rain and meltwater have created a playground for the rapidly growing community of canyoning enthusiasts. While this is a relatively new activity in the Rockies, there are pockets of well-established canyoneers in the United States and Europe. Only recently have professionals been able to become accredited canyoning guides in Canada. Whitegoat Falls is a popular small waterfall that is great for beginners and as an introduction to canyoning. There are much more adventurous descents throughout the David Thompson corridor and in Banff and Jasper national parks.

12. Unnamed Falls (Little Indian Falls)

LOCATION: Abraham Lake, AB
DRIVING DIFFICULTY: Easy
HIKING DIFFICULTY: Easy
HIKING DISTANCE: 3.0 km
HIKING TIME: 1 h

Driving directions

From the junction of Highway 11 and Stuart Street near Nordegg, drive west on Highway 11 for 46 km to the David Thompson Resort (signed). Turn left off the highway and into the resort, then keep to the left for day-use parking. Best to park up against the trees that parallel the highway so as not to interfere with guests at the lodge, campground, gas station and shop.

Hiking directions

From the parking area, walk into the campground and follow the outer loop in a clockwise direction. Keep an eye out for a sign on the left for Lake Trail. Descend this gravel road for a short distance, keeping an eye out for a lightly used trail on the left marked with flagging (1.0 km from the campground entrance). Follow this trail for 2.0 km to a small stream crossing above the waterfall. Cross the stream, then scramble down to the base of a small waterfall. Return the way you came.

Note: Aurum Lodge is private property. There are trails that continue beyond and above the falls that are near enough to the lodge that they should be avoided. There is no public parking or public trail access to the falls from Aurum Lodge.

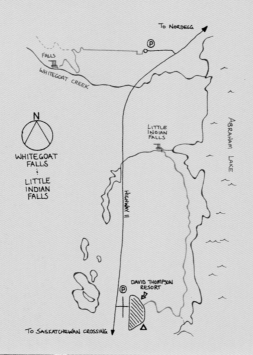

N

WHITEGOAT
FALLS
↓
LITTLE
INDIAN
FALLS

To NORDEGG

FALLS

WHITEGOAT CREEK

LITTLE
INDIAN
FALLS

ABRAHAM LAKE

HIGHWAY 11

DAVID THOMPSON
RESORT

To SASKATCHEWAN CROSSING

13. Siffleur Falls

LOCATION: Cline River, AB
DRIVING DIFFICULTY: Easy
HIKING DIFFICULTY: Easy
HIKING DISTANCE: 3.6 km
HIKING TIME: 1.5 h

As one of the few trails in the area marked by a sign, it only stands to reason that the place should be popular. And the Siffleur Falls hike is just that. Its popularity is well deserved, though, and the price of admission is low. This trail has a bit of everything: a suspension bridge, big views and big waterfalls. It is a must-see for everyone visiting the area.

Driving directions

From the junction of Highway 11 and Stuart Street near Nordegg, drive west on Highway 11 for 62 km to a junction on the left signed for Siffleur Falls. The parking lot is large, but it also fills up (relatively) quickly on weekends.

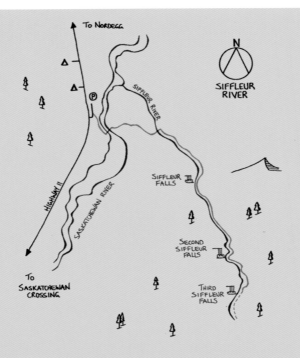

Hiking directions

From the parking area, follow a broad pathway for 500 m to a suspension bridge over the North Saskatchewan River. Continue on the boardwalk through a grassland and then along a wide trail to a bridge over the Siffleur River. Cross the bridge and then stay to the right. At 3.2 km there is a viewpoint along the edge of the canyon. Siffleur Falls is just a few hundred metres farther and can be viewed from platforms above the falls and over a narrowing in the canyon.

The noble marmot

The hoary marmot is the most common of the species that inhabit the Canadian Rockies, the yellow marmot being another. They are the largest member of the North American ground squirrel family and are known for their whistle, which echoes throughout the alpine. The Siffleur River and Siffleur Mountain were named by James Hector. Siffleur is French for "whistler" and these features were named for the high-pitched sound of the hoary marmot. Now that all the dots are connected, enjoy this classic David Thompson Country hike!

14. Second & Third Siffleur Falls

LOCATION: Cline River, AB
DRIVING DIFFICULTY: Easy
HIKING DIFFICULTY: Moderate
HIKING DISTANCE: 6.5 km
HIKING TIME: 2.5–3 h

While Siffleur Falls is the most captivating of the three, the hike to Third Siffleur Falls is an amazing day out. The trail sticks to the edge of a canyon high above the river, passing Second Falls en route to the end of the trail near the uppermost waterfall.

Driving directions

From the junction of Highway 11 and Stuart Street near Nordegg, drive west on Highway 11 for 62 km to a junction on the left signed for Siffleur Falls.

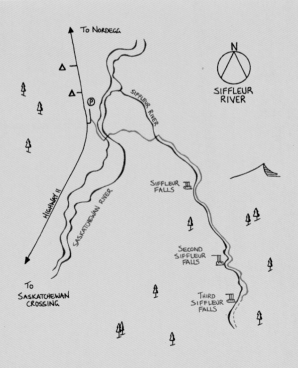

Hiking directions

From the parking area, follow a broad pathway for 500 m to a suspension bridge over the North Saskatchewan River. Continue on the boardwalk through a grassland and then along a wide trail to a bridge over the Siffleur River. Cross the bridge and then stay to the right, following the trail to Siffleur Falls at 3.6 km.

Shortly after Siffleur Falls, the trail gains elevation and climbs to the rim of the canyon. At 6.0 km Second Siffleur Falls is visible below but inaccessible. At 6.5 km a small stream intersects the trail and Third Siffleur Falls is visible from the riverbank. This is the best view of the falls and the recommended turnaround point. It is possible to continue with a short scramble up a steep dirt path to a vantage point above the waterfall. The end of the maintained trail is just beyond this, at the 7.0 km mark, with the Siffleur Wilderness Area beyond.

15. Thompson Creek Falls (Lower)

LOCATION: Cline River, AB
DRIVING DIFFICULTY: Easy
HIKING DIFFICULTY: Easy
HIKING DISTANCE: 1.0 km
HIKING TIME: 20 min

Thompson Creek Falls is a small cascade and a short, sweet hike if you need to stretch your legs or if you've given up on locating all the other trailheads along Highway 11. This mellow trail follows alongside the creek through a portion of forest burned in a 2014 wildfire.

Driving directions

From the junction of Highway 11 and Stuart Street near Nordegg, drive west on Highway 11 for 81 km to the Thompson Creek campground. You can either turn left into the campground and park at the day-use area, or continue to a small gravel parking area on the north side of the highway, just before (east of) the creek.

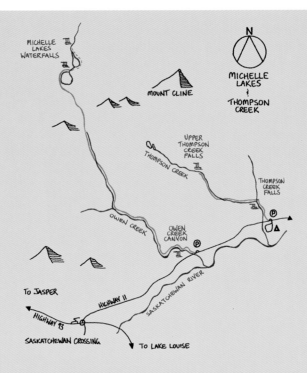

Hiking directions

From the parking area, pick up a well-used trail along the right-hand side of Thompson Creek. Follow through the scorched forest for 1.0 km to a log "bridge" over a creek and a small waterfall.

Camping in David Thompson Country

While Thompson Creek is a provincial recreation site and features developed campsites, toilet facilities, fire rings and picnic tables, much of David Thompson Country falls within a Public Land Use Zone (PLUZ) designation. While random camping is permitted in many areas, it is important to be up to date with boundaries, locations and the regulations for camping on public land. If you camp outside of maintained sites, it is equally important to practise the Leave No Trace principles, especially when it comes to disposing of human waste and garbage.

Restrictions for camping in PLUZ areas and PLRAs include:

- you must camp at least 1 km away from any provincial park, recreation site or Public Land Recreation Area (PLRA).

- in many PLUZes, you must camp at least 1 km from a roadway.

For more information on random backcountry camping and the various regulations for Public Land Use Zones and Public Land Recreation Areas, visit **alberta.ca/public-land-use-zones.aspx** and **alberta.ca/public-land-recreation-areas-and-trails.aspx**.

16. Thompson Creek Falls (Upper)

LOCATION: Cline River, AB
DRIVING DIFFICULTY: Easy
HIKING DIFFICULTY: Moderate
HIKING DISTANCE: 4.6 km
HIKING TIME: 2.5–3 h

Full disclosure: the hike to the upper waterfall on Thompson Creek is a grind. It gains nearly 500 metres of elevation, most of it in the final 2 km. There's a bit of deadfall along the way as well as some steep, side-sloping sections of the trail that will keep you on your toes. The hike will have you sweating, short of breath and with burning thighs, not to mention cursing the author for having included it in this guidebook. If it weren't absolutely worth seeing, it absolutely wouldn't be in the book... therefore you absolutely must go!

Driving directions

From the junction of Highway 11 and Stuart Street near Nordegg, drive west on Highway 11 for 81 km to the Thompson Creek campground. You can either turn left into the campground and park at the day-use area, or continue to a small gravel parking area on the north side of the highway, just before (east of) the creek.

Hiking directions

From the parking area, pick up a well-used trail along the right-hand side of Thompson Creek. Hike through the scorched forest for 1.0 km to a log "bridge" over a creek and a small waterfall. Cross the creek and continue along the trail another 150 m to a second log crossing. From here the trail follows along the left side of the creek and is occasionally indistinct as it wanders in and out of the creekbed. After 2.8 km the trail begins to climb steeply and steadily. At 4.0 km the waterfall becomes visible through the trees.

You've come this far, don't stop now. The last few hundred metres are a bit of a grunt, but with the waterfall in sight, you owe it to yourself to go the rest of the way.

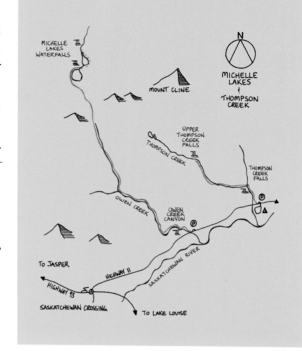

Elevation gain and hiking

This hike is a great example of how elevation gain affects time and travel. A 4.5 km walk on a flat roadway or trail can be expected to take most adults a little over an hour to complete. If that same 4.5 km walk also gains 300 metres of elevation (about 1,000 feet), you could reasonably plan to add another hour to your time.

While most hikes in this guide are simple and quick, there are a few that gain significant elevation along the way. If they do, that elevation is essential information for hikers to know. They can generally expect to take a little longer and exert themselves a little more. Hikers should bring extra water to make up for perspiration. Extra layering also becomes important, especially on a cool day. While you won't feel it while you're hiking, once you come to a stop and that damp, sweaty shirt cools off, you'll want something to throw over yourself until you start moving again.

17. Owen Creek Canyon

LOCATION: Cline River, AB
DRIVING DIFFICULTY: Easy
HIKING DIFFICULTY: Easy
HIKING DISTANCE: 750 m
HIKING TIME: 20 min

If you've ever visited Marble, Mistaya or Maligne canyons, this little-known trail is worthy of inclusion on that list. The Owen Creek trail is hiked as part of the Great Divide Trail and generally not on the radar for many day-hikers. It also lacks a signed trailhead and developed parking area, which has kept it rather obscure. But no more!!

Driving directions

From the junction of Highway 11 and Highway 93 at Saskatchewan Crossing, drive east on Highway 11 for 6 km to the Banff National Park boundary. A small driveway drops off the road on the left (north side of highway) behind a large Parks Canada sign with a bear warning. Follow the driveway down a short ways and park near the creek.

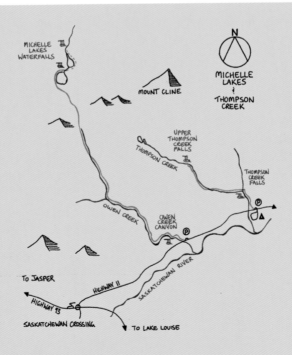

Hiking directions

From the parking area, a narrow trail enters the trees and follows along Owen Creek on its right-hand side. After 400 m the trail begins to climb steeply as the creek pours out of a narrow canyon flanked by high walls. Some 100 metres farther and just off the trail there is a viewpoint above a small waterfall that tumbles out of the canyon.

But wait, it gets better. Continue up the steep trail to the rim of the canyon. There are numerous places to look down into the narrow chasm and the bright-blue water churning below. About 750 m from the trailhead is the entry to the canyon where Owen Creek takes its initial plunge.

Exercise extreme caution around the edge of the canyon. Unlike the other Rockies attractions with similar features, there is no development or safeguards here to protect hikers. Always keep an eye on children and use extra caution if the trail is wet.

18. Michelle Lakes Waterfall

LOCATION: Cline River, AB
DRIVING DIFFICULTY: Easy
HIKING DIFFICULTY: Difficult
  (due to distance and elevation gain; overnight recommended)
HIKING DISTANCE: 13.3 km
HIKING TIME: 4–7 h

Possibly the premier hike in this guidebook, but not for the reasons you're thinking. The waterfall separating the upper and lower Michelle Lakes is nice, but it pales in comparison to the scenery high in this alpine paradise. Sound too good to be true? It's not... but the price of admission is high. The hike to Michelle Lakes is strenuous, gaining nearly 1100 metres of elevation to Owen Pass before descending to the lakes. Day hikers will have the advantage of light packs and can dispatch the trail at a faster pace but will have to hike all the way back out. Backpackers will only have to get to the lakes but will do so under the crushing weight of their overnight packs. So pick your poison.

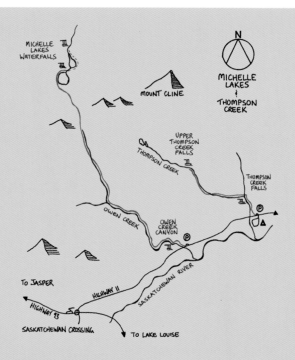

Driving directions

From the junction of Highway 11 and Highway 93 at Saskatchewan Crossing, drive east on Highway 11 for 6 km to the Banff National Park boundary. A small driveway drops off the road on the left-hand (north side of highway) behind a large Parks Canada sign with a bear warning. Follow the driveway down a short ways and park near the creek.

Hiking directions

From the parking area, a narrow trail goes into the trees and follows Owen Creek on its right-hand side. Pass Owen Creek Canyon as the trail climbs steeply before levelling out above. The next 4 km gain elevation gently but there are numerous obstacles, including deadfall and some trail erosion. Around the 5 km mark, the trail bends to the right and begins a long, steep ascent along the right-hand side of the creek, passing a few small cascades along the way.

At 7.5 km cross a small stream that connects with Owen Creek. The next 1.5 km are spent hopping back and forth over the creek,

following the path of least resistance. The trail is still well defined through this stretch. Around 8.5 km the pass will be visible at the far end of the valley. You'll want to aim for the lowest point in the saddle, toward the left-hand side of the pass. There is not much of a trail beyond this point as you travel through the bare, rocky landscape. Continue ascending to the pass at 10.5 km.

With the elevation gain complete, travel through the pass and descend into a basin. Upper Michelle Lake is out of sight to the right, hidden by a rib of rock. As you drop into the basin and round the corner, the lakes come into view. Reach the upper lake at 12.0 km. Continue on a trail along the shoreline in a clockwise direction. At the far end of the lake there are bear lockers for campers to store food. Beyond the bear lockers, a small headwall separates the two lakes, with

the waterfall splitting the cliff face. Stay to the right and locate a weakness in the cliff band, which is descended to the base of the waterfall and a couple of five-star campsites.

More to explore: Lower Michelle Lake and Lower Falls

From the base of the waterfall, you can continue to the far end of the lower lake via a faint trail travelling counter-clockwise around the shore. A small stream at the outlet of the lake plunges 300 metres down a headwall into the Waterfalls Creek valley. There isn't much of a view of the fall itself but the vista from the top of the headwall is breathtaking. Use an abundance of caution, as there is only air beneath you here.

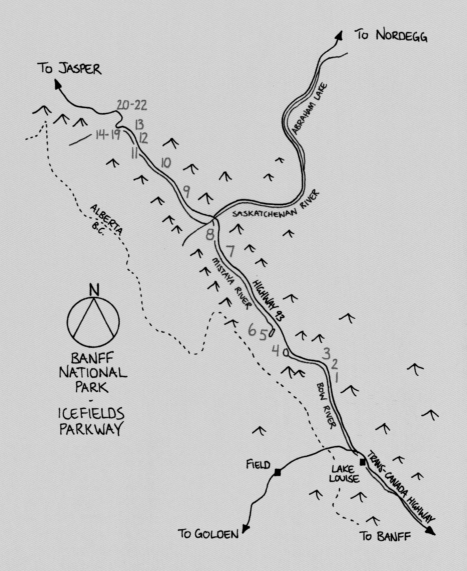

TO NORDEGG

TO JASPER

20-22
13
12
11
10
9
8
7
6 5
4
3 2
1

ABRAHAM LAKE

SASKATCHEWAN RIVER

ALBERTA
B.C.

MISTAYA RIVER

HIGHWAY 93

BOW RIVER

N

BANFF
NATIONAL
PARK
-
ICEFIELDS
PARKWAY

FIELD

LAKE
LOUISE

TRANS-CANADA HIGHWAY

TO GOLDEN

TO BANFF

CHAPTER 4

Banff National Park – Icefields Parkway

Banff National Park is the crown jewel of the Canadian national parks system and was the first park established in this fine country. The town of Banff is to Canada as Venice is to Italy or Santorini is to Greece: picturesque beyond compare and a natural attraction for visitors. In fact, the town was created solely with tourism in mind. With access to some of the most spectacular mountain scenery in the entire solar system, it is not difficult to see why people from all over the galaxy flock to these towering peaks, dazzling glaciers and sparkling lakes of Canada's flagship outdoor playground.

Waterfalls are in great abundance as towering walls of stone rise from the valley floors, many being capped with glaciers and snowfields that feed streams and creeks year-round. Here you'll find some of the most accessible hiking in the country, with numerous trailheads located along the Trans-Canada Highway. This makes Banff an ideal venue for families with small children or time constraints to take in many amazing short hikes with little effort or organization required.

Banff National Park can be accessed from five directions:

- from the southeast via the Trans-Canada Highway from Calgary and Canmore

- from the west via Highway 93S from Radium and Kootenay National Park

- from the northwest via the Trans-Canada Highway from Golden, Field and Yoho National Park

- from the north via Highway 93N from Jasper and Jasper National Park

- from the east via Highway 11, the David Thompson Highway, from Red Deer and Nordegg

All vehicles driving the Icefields Parkway require a park pass, which can be purchased at the park gates, visitor centres and some online sites. Most frontcountry and many backcountry campsites require reservations and a backcountry permit as well as the vehicle pass.

For more information contact the Banff National Park visitor centre:
pc.gc.ca/en/pn-np/ab/banff
224 Banff Ave, Banff, AB
(403) 762-1550
Camping reservations: 1-888-737-3783

1. Unnamed Waterfall (Hector Falls)

LOCATION: Banff National Park
DRIVING DIFFICULTY: Easy
HIKING DIFFICULTY: Easy
HIKING DISTANCE: 1.1 km
HIKING TIME: 20–30 min

Hector Creek will be a recognizable feature for climbers, mountaineers and skiers, less so for casual hikers. That said, the short stroll to the base of Hector Falls is a worthwhile outing that does not require a rope or crampons.

Driving directions

From the junction of the Trans-Canada Highway and Highway 93, drive north on Highway 93 for 20 km. Just after Hector Creek, turn in to a pullout on the left-hand (west) side of the highway (unsigned).

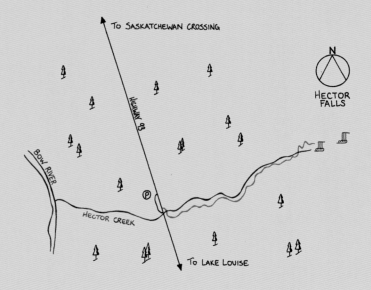

Hiking directions

From the parking area, cross Highway 93 to the south (right-hand) side of Hector Creek. Locate a well-used trail leading into the trees. The trail winds through the forest before breaking out into an open area below a headwall. Continue along the trail as it steepens to the base of the headwall and a waterfall pouring over a cliff band.

There is an upper tier of the waterfall that can be reached by continuing on the trail which ascends steeply beside the lower falls.

Rockies giants

Mount Hector is one of the 54 peaks whose summit elevation is 11,000 feet or higher, vaulting it into a collection of highly regarded mountaineering objectives. This list includes the most prominent peaks in the Canadian Rockies such as Mount Robson, Mount Columbia, Mount Temple and Mount Assiniboine to name just a few. These high mountains have become valuable destinations for the mountaineering and climbing community, specifically for their height and significance. Mount Hector was the second "11,000er" to be summited, in 1895, after Mount Temple was climbed the year before.

Hector Creek is used by mountaineers and skiers to access Mount Hector's North Glacier, the most common route up the mountain. The waterfall is frozen and snow-covered in the winter.

2. Unnamed Waterfalls (Noseeum Creek Waterfalls)

LOCATION: Banff National Park
DRIVING DIFFICULTY: Easy
HIKING DIFFICULTY: Easy
HIKING DISTANCE: 2.0 km
HIKING TIME: 45 min

Noseeum Creek is a seldom-used drainage in the summertime, save for a handful of people exploring Noseeum Lake or the lofty summit of Noseeum Peak. It is a much more popular zone in the wintertime and provides access to some steep backcountry skiing. The melting snow fuels side-by-side cascades down the headwall at the back of a subalpine basin. While this is an area you can explore without the crowds, the price for that solitude is the lack of a well-maintained trail, not to mention that what trail there is can occasionally be tricky to locate.

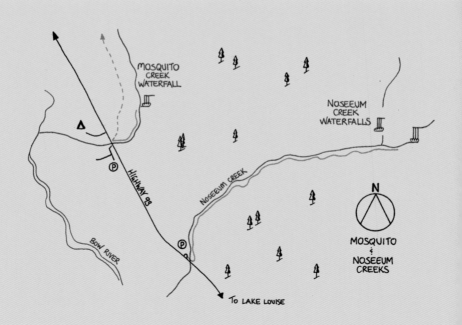

Driving directions

From the junction of the Trans-Canada Highway and Highway 93, drive north on Highway 93 for 22.5 km and turn right, into a small pullout on the right-hand (east) side of the highway. A large sign there, Mosquito – 1 km, makes a good landmark.

Hiking directions

From the parking area, cross over Noseeum Creek above the culvert or on the highway. Locate a lightly used but obvious trail along the right-hand (south) side of the creek. After 700 m, the trail enters talus rock slopes and becomes indistinct at times. It stays close to the creek, never more than 10–15 m away. If you find yourself wandering up the rocks and off the trail, chances are it is below you and closer to the creek. There is the occasional cairn to help guide the way.

After you've hiked 1.1 km, the headwall and waterfalls become visible at the back of the basin. Cross a small stream at 1.5 km and continue through the rocky basin for another 500 m or to the base of the waterfalls. At this point the trail is generally non-existent through sprawling fields of talus rock. Watch your step.

3. Unnamed Waterfall (Mosquito Creek Falls)

LOCATION: Banff National Park
DRIVING DIFFICULTY: Easy
HIKING DIFFICULTY: Easy
HIKING DISTANCE: 500 m
HIKING TIME: 15 min

This is an amazing short jaunt close to the road that is often missed by hikers heading up Mosquito Creek. It is not on the main trail, but instead follows the drainage to where Mosquito Creek slips through a small canyon. In spite of its daunting name, the mosquitos are actually in relatively short supply here. Perhaps Mosquito Creek was an intentional misnomer designed to keep tourists moving northward to Bow Lake?

Driving directions

From the junction of the Trans-Canada Highway and Highway 93, drive north on Highway 93 for 23.5 km. Turn left (west) into the trailhead parking area (signed for Mosquito Creek Hostel). If this parking

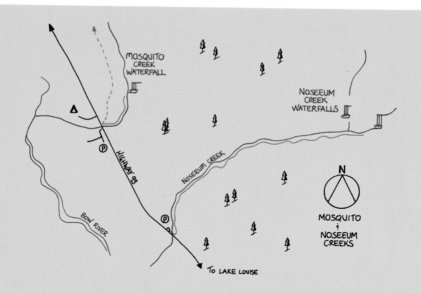

lot is full, additional parking may be available at the Mosquito Creek campground day-use area, the next turnoff to the north.

Hiking directions

From the parking area, cross Highway 93 and locate a trailhead kiosk on the left (north) side of Mosquito Creek. Instead of starting up the main pathway at the kiosk, head towards the creek. A lightly used trail follows along the left-hand side of the creek. After a brief, steep scramble up a loose slope, the trail levels off again. A small waterfall in a narrow canyon will be visible soon after.

More to explore: backpacking trips from Mosquito Creek

Mosquito Creek is a popular staging area for backcountry hiking and backpacking trips to North Molar Pass, Fish Lakes, Devon Lakes and beyond. The area has a number of backcountry campsites which facilitate access deep into this beautiful, wild corner of Banff National Park. From the trailhead it is 5.5 km to the Mosquito Creek campground and 14.8 km to the Fish Lakes campground. Trips into the Clearwater Pass and Devon Lakes area are a more serious undertaking, generally requiring a multi-day trip. There are numerous hiking guides and online resources to research trips of this nature in greater detail.

4. Bow Glacier Falls

LOCATION: Banff National Park
DRIVING DIFFICULTY: Easy
HIKING DIFFICULTY: Easy
HIKING DISTANCE: 4.5 km
HIKING TIME: 2 h

Bow Glacier Falls looks tantalizingly close to onlookers drooling over the scenery along Bow Lake. While the waterfall is deceptively distant, it is a reasonable half day-hike to see it up close and well worth slipping away from the gallery of people oohing and ahhing their way around the lakeshore.

Driving directions

From the junction of the Trans-Canada Highway and Highway 93, drive north on Highway 93 for 35.2 km. Turn left into the signed parking area for Bow Lake and Num-Ti-Jah Lodge.

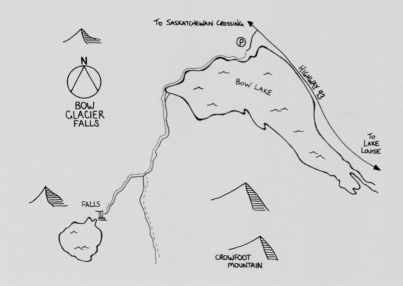

Hiking directions

From the parking area for Bow Lake and Num-Ti-Jah Lodge, follow a trail along the shoreline of the lake in a counter-clockwise direction. After reaching the far shore, pick your way across a large gravel flat at the west end of the lake. The trail then ascends briefly into the trees to a junction with the Bow Hut route. Stay right to continue to Bow Glacier Falls. At 3.7 km the trail ascends a rocky moraine with great views of the 150-metre waterfall. If you want to get a little closer, follow a less-used path through the rubbly basin to near the base of the falls.

A river is born

It is here, where Bow Glacier Falls tumbles out from the ice above, that one of Canada's longest river systems begins its journey. After a short rest at Bow Lake, the Bow River continues south through the Rockies before turning east and joining the Oldman River to form the South Saskatchewan River on its journey east. Near Prince Albert, it joins forces with the North Saskatchewan River and carries on as the Saskatchewan River to Lake Winnipeg, 1939 km away from Bow Glacier.

5. Lower Caldron Falls

LOCATION: Banff National Park
DRIVING DIFFICULTY: Easy
HIKING DIFFICULTY: Difficult (due to icy cold creek crossings)
HIKING DISTANCE: 5.6 km
HIKING TIME: 2.0–2.5 h

> **Caution: This hike is classified as difficult due to uneven terrain, creek crossings and occasional route finding. It is not recommended for children or inexperienced hikers. For those heading to Caldron Falls and beyond to Caldron Lake, sturdy footwear and spare socks are a must, as well as being prepared for a long day out.**

Lower Caldron Falls is completely hidden from view until you're brushing right up against it. It is a spectacular waterfall tucked away in an alcove that is a worthy objective in itself.

Driving directions

From the junction of the Trans-Canada Highway and Highway 93, drive north on Highway 93 for 40 km. Turn left into the signed parking area for Peyto Lake Viewpoint.

Hiking directions

From parking, follow the paved pathway to the Peyto Lake viewing platform. Leave the pavement just after the viewpoint and descend steeply through forest all the way down to Peyto Lake. After crossing the frigid waters of Peyto Creek, proceed west through a gravel outwash on the west side of the lake. At the far end of the gravel flats, locate a trail along the right-hand side of the creek. The trail bobs and weaves beside the creek, occasionally ascending into the trees only to drop back down again. The path is occasionally washed out and requires careful footwork. At 4.4 km, begin ascending through boulders and talus slopes, with Caldron Creek below you on the left. At 5.6 km, reach Lower Caldron Falls.

Note: Many trip reports and hiking guidebooks reference a log footbridge over Peyto Creek and a hand cable for crossing Caldron Creek. Both of those have long since been washed away, so don't squander your time searching for them. Currently, Parks Canada does not appear to have any intention of replacing them.

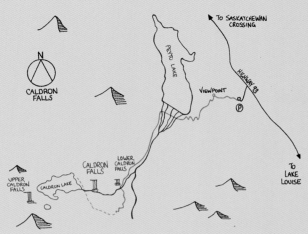

The Man, The Myth, The Legend

Peyto Lake is named for Ebenezer William Peyto, one of the first national park wardens and a renowned guide and outfitter. Among many colourful stories told about "Wild Bill" is one where he trapped a lynx and carried it on his back into the town of Banff. It is said that he released the cat in a saloon, at which point the patrons fled and Bill Peyto would enjoy his drink in solitude. When finished, he took the animal and presented it to the curator of the Banff Park Museum. This is only one of many tales featuring the historical figure, some true, some maybe less true. Peyto worked as a warden from 1913 to 1936, his tenure interrupted only by his service in the First World War.

6. Caldron Falls

LOCATION: Banff National Park
DRIVING DIFFICULTY: Easy
HIKING DIFFICULTY: Easy (to Peyto Lake Viewpoint); DIFFICULT (to Caldron Falls)
HIKING DISTANCES: 700 m (to Peyto Lake Viewpoint); 6.0 km (to Caldron Falls)
HIKING TIMES: 10 min (to Peyto Lake Viewpoint); 2.5–3.0 h (to Caldron Falls)

> Caution: This hike is classified as difficult due to uneven terrain, creek crossings and occasional route finding. It is not recommended for children or inexperienced hikers. For those heading to Caldron Falls and beyond to Caldron Lake, sturdy boots and spare socks are a must, as well as being prepared for a long day out. Alternatively, the falls can be viewed from a distance at the popular Peyto Lake viewing platform, just a short jaunt from the parking area.

Driving directions

From the junction of the Trans-Canada Highway and Highway 93, drive north on Highway 93 for 40 km. Turn left into the signed parking area for Peyto Lake Viewpoint.

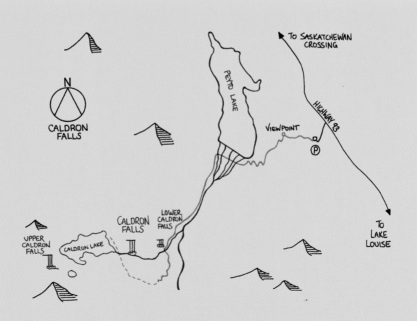

Hiking directions

From the parking area, follow a paved trail to a large viewing platform.

For those hiking to the falls, leave the pavement just after the viewpoint and descend a well-used trail through forest all the way down to Peyto Lake. After crossing the frigid waters of Peyto Creek, proceed west through a gravel outwash on the west side of the lake (no trail). At the far end of the gravel flats, locate a faint trail along the right-hand side of the creek. The path bobs and weaves beside the creek, occasionally ascending into the trees only to drop back down again, the trail is occasionally washed out and requires careful footwork. At 4.4 km, begin ascending through boulders and talus slopes, with the Caldron Creek below you on the left. At 5.6 km, reach Lower Caldron Falls.

From the lower falls, find a safe place to cross Caldron Creek. This will be the crux of the hike and may not be possible if the stream is running high. Once across the creek, a well-used trail climbs a moraine and Caldron Falls comes into view shortly after, 6.0 km from the trailhead.

More to explore: Caldron Lake and Upper Caldron Falls

As you continue up the moraine, Caldron Falls slips from view. From here, a side-sloping traverse cuts across a steep scree slope. This is a no fall zone: use extra caution and do not attempt this traverse if it's snow-covered. Once across the scree traverse, descend slightly before crossing a small boulder field and then continue on to the very picturesque Caldron Lake. Upper Caldron Falls is a tall cataract plunging over the headwall that separates Peyto Peak and Mistaya Mountain. It is 8.0 km from the parking area to Caldron Lake.

7. Bison Falls

LOCATION: Banff National Park
DRIVING DIFFICULTY: Easy
HIKING DIFFICULTY: Moderate
HIKING DISTANCE: 1.5 km
HIKING TIME: 45–60 min

Bison Falls is a little-known feature that is visible from the Icefields Parkway only by the keenest of eyes. A fleeting glimpse of the waterfall reveals an impressive plunge off a rocky mantel. There is no formal trail to the falls, so in order to keep the impact as low as possible, the recommended route is up a dry stream bed before it connects with a trail used by ice climbers.

Driving directions

From the junction of the Trans-Canada Highway and Highway 93, drive north on Highway 93 for 63.5 km. Turn right into a large unsigned pullout.

Alternatively, from the junction of Highway 93 and the David Thompson Highway (Highway 11), drive south on Highway 93 for 11.5 km to the parking area, which will be on the left.

Hiking directions

From the parking area, walk north on the shoulder of the highway for about 250 m. Locate a small, dry, rocky stream bed off the right-hand (east) side of the road. Drop down into the stream bed and follow for 750 m until it meets Bison Creek. Just before the creek, a faint climber's trail marked by a cairn ascends steeply out from the rocks and into the trees. Some scrambling may be required. Follow the climber's trail for 500 m as it ascends high above Bison Creek, passing another large waterfall on the way. These directions are to a view of Bison Falls; travel beyond this viewpoint is not recommended.

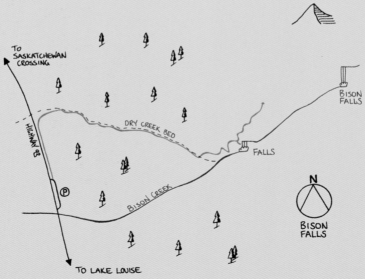

TO
SASKATCHEWAN
CROSSING

DRY CREEK BED

BISON
FALLS

FALLS

HIGHWAY 93

Ⓟ

BISON CREEK

N

BISON
FALLS

TO LAKE LOUISE

8. Mistaya Canyon

LOCATION: Banff National Park
DRIVING DIFFICULTY: Easy
HIKING DIFFICULTY: Easy
HIKING DISTANCE: 500 m
HIKING TIME: 10 min

The brilliant blue waters of the Mistaya River etching a pathway through a deep, narrow groove in the earth is a captivating sight. With the hulking mass of Mount Sarbach providing the backdrop, the scene is nothing less than postcard worthy. In fact, you'll likely find this very photo gracing postcard racks in gift shops throughout western Canada. Fortunately, with a trip to Mistaya Canyon and some basic knowledge of your cell phone's camera, you can make your own postcards!

Driving directions

From the junction of the Trans-Canada Highway and Highway 93, drive north on Highway 93 for 70 km. Turn left into the signed parking area for Mistaya Canyon.

Alternatively, from the junction of Highway 93 and the David Thompson Highway (Highway 11), drive south on Highway 93 for 5.2 km to the parking area on the right.

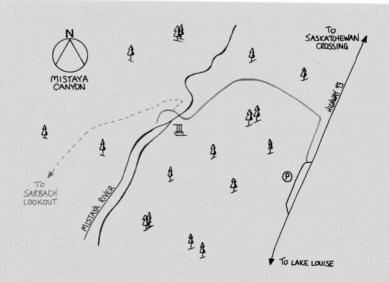

Hiking directions

From the parking area, a well-used pathway descends gently through the forest for about 500 m before crossing a bridge over a deep slot canyon. Across the bridge you can access many rocky outcroppings alongside the rim of the canyon. Use caution on the rocks, as they can become slippery when wet and there are no barriers in place.

Grizzlies in Banff National Park

The grizzly bear is the most recognizable, respected and feared animal in the Canadian Rockies. Yet, there are only an estimated 65 that currently roam Banff National Park. While the grizzly bear has no natural predators, their numbers continue to decline due to accidents with trains or highway vehicles. Unfortunately, due to the harsh mountain environment, they also reproduce more slowly than black bears or grizzlies in other regions.

The word Mistaya originates from the Cree language and means "grizzly bear."

9. Unnamed Falls (Lower Lady Wilson Falls)

LOCATION: Banff National Park
DRIVING DIFFICULTY: Easy
HIKING DIFFICULTY: Moderate (no trail)
HIKING DISTANCE: 600 m
HIKING TIME: 20 min

As you drive north from Saskatchewan Crossing, the impressive west flanks of Mount Wilson, Mount Coleman and Cirrus Mountain tower above you. These three peaks are draped with tassels of small waterfalls, many flowing only as the snow thaws in late spring and early summer. A handful do flow year-round where glaciers and lakes provide sufficient water. Access to these waterfalls is fairly restricted, with limited parking opportunities and even fewer trails. One of the falls which can be accessed with little difficulty is the lower cascade of Lady Wilson Falls (which is easily seen high above the roadway).

It should be stated that while this hike has no designated trail, the approach to the waterfall is the rocky banks of the stream bed which provides a sturdy and resilient surface to walk on and therefore poses no risk of damaging vegetation.

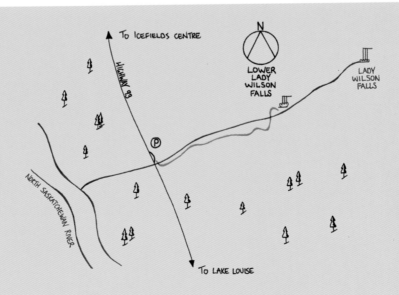

Driving directions

From the junction of Highway 93 and the David Thompson Highway (Highway 11), drive north on Highway 93 for 8.8 km. There is a raised portion of the highway that crosses a wide gravel stream bed. Park in a widening on the right-hand side of the highway.

Hiking directions

From the parking area, walk along either bank of a small stream; the right-hand side seems to offer easier travel. As the falls come into view, near their base, cross over to the left side of the creek and scramble up a short, steep slope to the foot of this small waterfall.

10. Norman Creek Falls

LOCATION: Banff National Park
DRIVING DIFFICULTY: Easy
HIKING DIFFICULTY: Easy
HIKING DISTANCE: 1.0 km
HIKING TIME: 20 min

The Norman Creek trail is the gateway to a number of classic backcountry locations, including Norman Lake, Pinto Lake, Sunset Pass and Sunset Lookout, and offers both day hikes and backpacking opportunities. Before you lace up those boots, though, there is a caveat, namely the more than 500 vertical metres of elevation gain from the trailhead to Norman Lake. The good news is that Norman Creek Falls is reached with only 20 per cent of the effort.

UNNAMED FALLS NEAR NORMAN LAKE

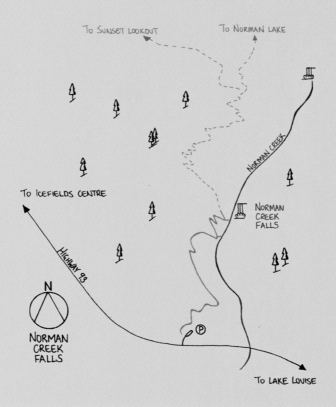

To Sunset Lookout

To Norman Lake

Norman Creek

Norman Creek Falls

To Icefields Centre

N

Highway 93

Norman Creek Falls

To Lake Louise

Driving directions

From the junction of Highway 93 and the David Thompson Highway (Highway 11), drive north on Highway 93 for 16.5 km. As the road descends to run alongside the North Saskatchewan River, there is a parking area and trailhead on the right-hand side of the highway, signed for Norman Creek.

Hiking directions

From parking, follow the well-used trail for Norman Lake for 1 km. A number of switchbacks make up this trail, and elevation is gained rapidly from the valley floor. At the corner of one switchback, Norman Creek can be heard beyond the trail. Two short spurs off the main trail lead to views of Norman Creek Falls.

NORMAN CREEK FALLS

Stay on the trail!!

There are a number of temptations to cut corners en route to Norman Lake, 32 to be relatively precise. Due to the required elevation gain, the trail switchbacks repeatedly. It can be enticing to shortcut these zig-zags to save time and distance, but such actions damage vegetation and thus cause excessive erosion, which is butt-ugly. These shortcuts are also steep and become very slippery, making them dangerous to boot. Parks Canada has gone to great lengths to rehabilitate these portions of the trail. Let's help them with that work and stick to established trails.

As a side note, many waterfalls were omitted from this book where they could not be accessed by way of a developed, sanctioned or established trail. Some hikes outside national and provincial park boundaries may feature brief sections of bushwhacking when it is safe to do so. We hope you as the reader employ the same ethics and standards in your outdoor pursuits.

11. Matchstick Falls

LOCATION: Banff National Park
DRIVING DIFFICULTY: Easy
HIKING DIFFICULTY: Easy
HIKING DISTANCE: 550 m
HIKING TIME: 10 min

A little-known waterfall on the North Saskatchewan River is Matchstick Falls. After the spring thaw, the water level drops and the river turns a vibrant shade of turquoise. On approach, the river slides quietly alongside a sandy and gravelly shore before it is violently shoved through a narrow gap in the rock. The riverbank is a great place to sit down with a snack and dip the toes.

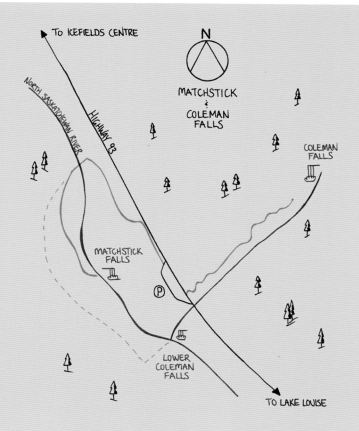

Driving directions

From the junction of the Trans-Canada Highway and Highway 93, drive north on Highway 93 for 99.3 km. Turn left into a large, unsigned pullout on the left-hand (west) side of the highway. This is the Cirrus Mountain viewpoint.

Hiking directions

From the parking area, walk north along the left (west) shoulder of the highway for 100 m. Leave the highway at an old, decommissioned gravel road and descend to the river (200 m). Cross an old concrete bridge, then look to your left for a faint trail or path of least resistance to descend to the river. Follow the riverbed for 200 m to large slabs of rock overlooking a small waterfall where the river narrows.

More to explore: Coleman Falls and Lower Coleman Falls

From the parking area, look up. That behemoth above you is Coleman Falls. It is possible for the excessively ambitious to reach these falls via a steep climber's trail. This is generally used by mountaineers attempting routes on Cirrus Mountain and Mount Coleman. There are few redeeming qualities to this hike. The trail is undeveloped, strewn with deadfall, and climbs at a nearly unreasonable grade.

Lower Coleman Falls is just below the south end of the parking area and can be heard from there. To view this waterfall, follow the directions above for Matchstick Falls. After leaving the highway, follow the old road for 600 m until roughly across from the south end of the parking area. A short, 50-metre bushwhack (indistinct trail) leads to the edge of a canyon across from a gorgeous cascading waterfall that falls directly into the North Saskatchewan River.

12. Unnamed Falls (Polar Circus)

LOCATION: Banff National Park
DRIVING DIFFICULTY: Easy
HIKING DIFFICULTY: Easy
HIKING DISTANCE: 500 m
HIKING TIME: 10 min

Look up. Higher. Higher. Higher. Polar Circus is a sliver of water that ricochets nearly 600 vertical metres down to the valley bottom from a plateau high on the flanks of Cirrus Mountain. Although the hike only takes you to the base of this immense waterfall, it can be seen nearly in its entirety from the road. It plummets through a gash in a towering wall of limestone in a series of steps and drops.

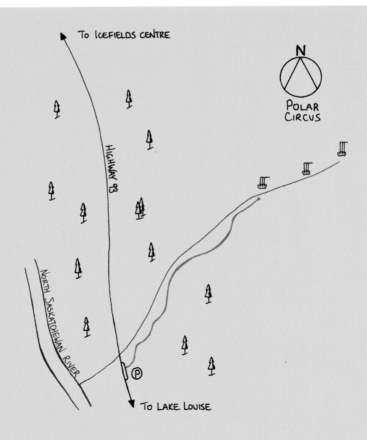

Driving directions

From the junction of the Trans-Canada Highway and Highway 93, drive north on Highway 93 for 101 km. Pull into a small, unsigned pullout on the right-hand (east) side of the highway just before a small creek crossing.

Hiking directions

From the parking area, follow a lightly used trail along the right-hand (south) side of the creek for 400 m. The trail then drops into a rocky creekbed. Follow for an additional 100 m to near the base of the lower tiers of the waterfall. At this point, the rocky banks bulge into the creek, preventing further progress. Travel beyond this point is not advised.

Polar Circus – the ice climb

Polar Circus borders on the mythical in the ice-climbing community. Its reputation as a difficult and often dangerous wall remains, decades after the first ascent of it. However, part of its infamy is also tied to tragedy, as it has claimed the lives of numerous climbers over the years, including the legendary John Lauchlan.

13. Weeping Wall

LOCATION: Banff National Park
DRIVING DIFFICULTY: Easy
HIKING DIFFICULTY: Easy
HIKING DISTANCE: 500 m
HIKING TIME: 10 min

The Weeping Wall is one of the most popular roadside stops in Banff National Park. Most visitors are content to roll down their car windows and snap their photos from the highway, unaware that one can hike right to the base of the wall for a shower. The wall weeps the most in the springtime when Cirrus Mountain is shedding its snow, resulting in numerous cascades tumbling down the thousand-foot-high cliff face. It is also incredibly dramatic during the winter when the wall freezes into a massive fortification of ice, although you can leave your towel and rubber ducky on the dashboard and forget the shower.

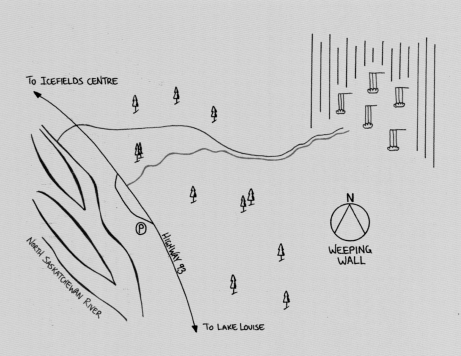

Driving directions

From the junction of the Trans-Canada Highway and Highway 93, drive north on Highway 93 for 103.5 km. Pull into a largish parking area on the left-hand side of the highway, signed for Weeping Wall.

Hiking directions

From the parking area, carefully cross the highway and locate a well-used trail that leads directly to the base of the cliffs.

In the wintertime, this is a popular venue for ice climbers. Give them a wide berth, as it is not uncommon for chunks of ice to come flying down from above.

14. Mistashu Falls

LOCATION: Banff National Park
DRIVING DIFFICULTY: Easy
HIKING DIFFICULTY: Easy
HIKING DISTANCE: 200 m
HIKING TIME: 5 min

This seldom seen and rarely visited waterfall has generally only been on the radar for the most avid of waterfall chasers. It can be seen from the Icefields Parkway for only a fleeting moment and with a keen eye. This is yet another waterfall that is more familiar to the ice-climbing community, but it's well worth a stop in the summertime for a look at one of the lesser-known sites near the highway.

Driving directions

From the junction of the Trans-Canada Highway and Highway 93, drive north on Highway 93 for 105.8 km. Park in a small, unsigned pullout on the left-hand side of the highway.

Hiking directions

From the parking area, cross the highway and walk on the shoulder heading south for about 50 m. Locate a game trail heading into the trees which quickly leads to views of this two-tiered waterfall. While there are more waterfalls farther upstream, the game trails dissipate quickly once in the trees. Travel beyond the view of Mistashu Falls is discouraged to prevent damage to vegetation in the park.

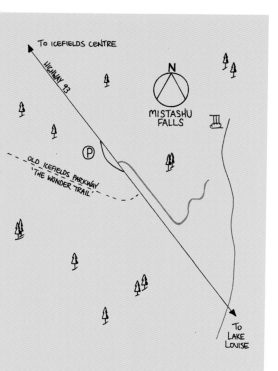

15. Nigel Falls

LOCATION: Banff National Park
DRIVING DIFFICULTY: Easy
HIKING DIFFICULTY: Easy
HIKING DISTANCE: 2.0 km
HIKING TIME: 30–40 min

Ever wonder what was below the bridge that towers high above Nigel Creek? Yeah, me too, until recently. Since the bridge has been in a perpetual state of construction and reconstruction since the dawn of time, pedestrian access to the bridge has been restricted from that point forward. A much better way to see Nigel Falls is a hike along the old Wonder Trail, the original Icefields highway.

Driving directions

From the junction of the Trans-Canada Highway and Highway 93, drive north on Highway 93 for 108.3 km. You will notice a small roadway leaving the Icefields Parkway on the left-hand side. Drive 800 m farther to the Big Bend parking area, turn around and head back south on the highway so you can safely exit into the old Wonder Trail parking area (unsigned). Parking is very limited here, with room for only a handful of vehicles, so make sure when you park you are not restricting the ability of others to back out and leave.

Hiking directions

From the parking area, walk past the barricade over an old bridge and follow the decommissioned gravel road for 1.7 km. When the road meets Nigel Creek, cross the bridge and pick up a well-used trail on the left that follows along the right-hand side of Nigel Creek. Hike an additional 300 m to a great view of Nigel Falls. At this point the creek will bar any further travel.

More to explore: Nigel Pass

While the short hike to Nigel Falls highlights an impressive waterfall along Nigel Creek, the alpine pass by the same name is more recognizable by hikers. The trailhead for Nigel Pass is actually high above the Big Bend, closer to the Icefields Centre, so let's address that little detail first.

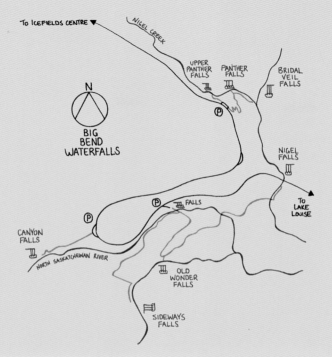

The hike to Nigel Pass is 7.2 km one way and gains about 350 metres in elevation. Once there, you will have expansive views of the Upper Brazeau River basin, the Nigel Creek valley, mountains, meadows and tarns. Allow most of a day (5–6 h) for this very worthwhile hike.

16. Old Wonder Falls

LOCATION: Banff National Park
DRIVING DIFFICULTY: Easy
HIKING DIFFICULTY: Easy
HIKING DISTANCE: 700 m
HIKING TIME: 15 min

Old Wonder Falls is visible from the Icefields Parkway near the bridge over Nigel Creek. From a distance, this thing looks like a beast of a waterfall. Once you're up close and personal with it, it is actually much tamer, as the creek is tumbling down a heap of boulders rather than rocketing over a cliff. It is named for the Wonder Trail, which was the name given to the original iteration of the Icefields Parkway – the single-lane gravel road that connected Jasper to Lake Louise.

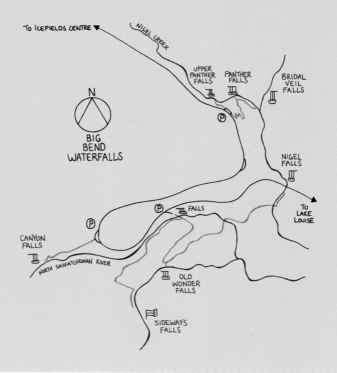

Driving directions

From the junction of the Trans-Canada Highway and Highway 93, drive north on Highway 93 for 108.3 km. You will notice a small roadway leaving the Icefields Parkway on the left-hand side. Drive 800 m farther to the Big Bend parking area, then turn around and head back south on the highway so you can safely exit into the Old Wonder Trail parking area (unsigned). Parking is very limited here, with room for only a handful of vehicles, so make sure when you park you are not restricting the ability of others to back out and leave.

Hiking directions

From the parking area, walk past the barricade over an old bridge and follow the decommissioned gravel road for 600 m. Old Wonder Falls becomes visible through the trees at a bend in the road. A handful of trails then descend towards the creek.

17. Sideways Falls

LOCATION: Banff National Park
DRIVING DIFFICULTY: Easy
HIKING DIFFICULTY: Easy
HIKING DISTANCE: 1.3 km
HIKING TIME: 30 min

If you stand in the Big Bend parking lot and look to the south, there is an odd waterfall that seems to corkscrew out of a gash in the side of a mountain and literally appears to be sideways upon liftoff. "Oblique," "athwart" and "crabwise" obviously didn't gain approval from the authorities naming waterfalls.

Driving directions

From the junction of the Trans-Canada Highway and Highway 93, drive north on Highway 93 for 108.3 km. You will notice a small road leaving the Icefields Parkway on the left-hand side. Drive 800 m farther to the Big Bend parking area, then turn around and head back south on the highway so you can safely exit into the Old Wonder Trail parking area (unsigned). Parking is very limited here, with room for only a handful of vehicles, so make sure when you park you are not restricting the ability of others to back out and exit.

Hiking directions

From the parking area, walk past the barricade and over an old bridge. Immediately after the bridge, find a trail to the right which travels along the left-hand side of the North Saskatchewan River. Hike for 500 m

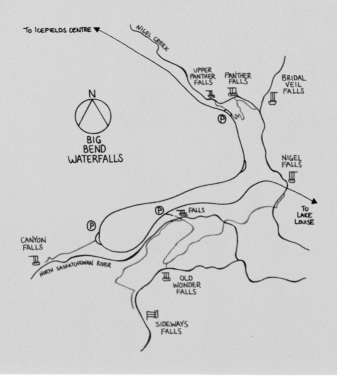

until you come to a decommissioned road. Follow this road for an additional 250 m until it opens up in a large gravel flat. At a Y junction, stay to the left and begin looking for a boot-beaten trail leading into the trees on the left, marked with a cairn. Take this trail for 200 m until you come to another creek. Upon reaching the creek, stay to the right and follow a faint trail along the right-hand side of the creek for another 150–200 m until the falls are in view.

The road to Saskatchewan Glacier

The gravel road along the North Saskatchewan River was commissioned in 1942 to access the tongue of Saskatchewan Glacier for the purpose of training United States soldiers. Good thing they didn't wait any longer. Saskatchewan Glacier retreats an average of 25–30 m per year and has diminished by about 1.2 km since 1940 and more than 2.0 km since the late 1800s.

18. North Saskatchewan Falls

LOCATION: Banff National Park
DRIVING DIFFICULTY: Easy
HIKING DIFFICULTY: Easy
HIKING DISTANCE: about 20 m
HIKING TIME: about zero min

Ever seen an entire river disappear? No magic here, the North Saskatchewan is literally swallowed whole by a gash in the rock no bigger than your own mouth. Alright, fine, slight exaggeration...

Driving directions

From the junction of the Trans-Canada Highway and Highway 93, drive north on Highway 93 for 108.3 km. You will notice a small roadway leaving the Icefields Parkway on the left-hand side. Drive 800 m farther to the Big Bend parking area, turn around and head back south on the highway so you can safely exit into the Old Wonder

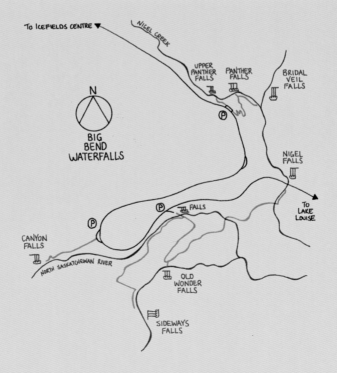

Trail parking area (unsigned). Parking is very limited here, with room for only a handful of vehicles, so make sure when you park you are not restricting the ability of others to back out and leave.

Hiking directions

From the parking area, walk straight down to the river. Don't get swallowed...

19. Unnamed Waterfall (Canyon Falls)

LOCATION: Banff National Park
DRIVING DIFFICULTY: Easy
HIKING DIFFICULTY: Easy
HIKING DISTANCE: 500 m
HIKING TIME: 15 min

Note: The *World Waterfall Database* refers to this waterfall as Middle North Saskatchewan Falls.

Without a signed parking area and trail, people often wonder why vehicles are lined up at the base of the curve on Highway 93's "Big Bend." Canyon Falls is the answer to that riddle: a narrow chasm where the pristine headwaters of the North Saskatchewan River start their journey eastward to Hudson Bay. The blue waters are only minutes from having melted from the toe of Saskatchewan Glacier, just a few kilometres upstream.

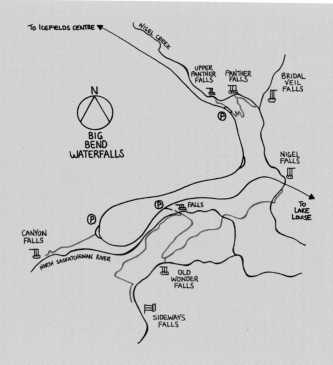

Driving directions

From the junction of Highway 93 and Highway 11 (Saskatchewan Crossing), drive north on Highway 93 for 35 km to an unsigned parking area on the west side of the highway at the bottom of the "Big Bend."

Hiking directions

From the parking area, head west through a gravel flat, keeping to the right of the river. Where the river enters a dark canyon, hike up a short, steep slope through the trees to a rocky rim perched above the small gorge.

20. *Bridal Veil Falls*

LOCATION: Banff National Park
DRIVING DIFFICULTY: Easy
HIKING DIFFICULTY: Easy
HIKING DISTANCE: 400 m
HIKING TIME: 10 min

If they were handing out yearbook awards for waterfalls in the Rockies, Bridal Veil would win "Most Likely to be Driven Right Past by Unsuspecting Motorists." Most pullouts and parking areas in Banff National Park are signed, which makes navigating quite simple, but this stop along the Icefields Parkway would be one of the exceptions. Keep a sharp eye out.

Driving directions

From the junction of Highway 93 and Highway 11 (Saskatchewan Crossing), drive north on Highway 93 for 36 km to a large, unsigned parking area on the east side of the highway at the top of the "Big Bend."

Hiking directions

After parking, walk south along the edge of the vast lot and locate a brown Parks Canada trail sign for Panther Falls and Bridal Veil Falls. The well-used pathway descends from there with constant views through the trees of the 366-metre-high cascade. While the best viewpoint may actually be from the parking area near the highway, there are good looks at it all along the pathway. The primary viewpoint is roughly 400 m from the trailhead. Don't stop here, though. Just around the corner is the thundering Panther Falls!

So many Bridal Veils

In the United States, there are 39 cataracts named Bridal Veil Falls. Canada has eight, including one in Quebec that translates directly to Bridal Veil Falls. So if your internet blows up with this name in the search field, don't worry about your Wi-Fi... you've simply been overloaded with search results.

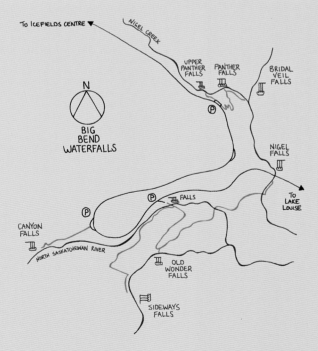

21. Panther Falls

LOCATION: Banff National Park
DRIVING DIFFICULTY: Easy
HIKING DIFFICULTY: Easy
HIKING DISTANCE: 500 m
HIKING TIME: 10 min

These may be the best two-for-one waterfall deal on the Icefields Parkway: Bridal Veil Falls and Panther Falls. While the former is easily viewed from an unsigned parking area just off the highway, the latter is tucked out of sight and only visible upon arrival.

Driving directions

From the junction of Highway 93 and Highway 11 (Saskatchewan Crossing), drive north on Highway 93 for 36 km to a large, unsigned parking area on the east side of the highway at the top of the "Big Bend."

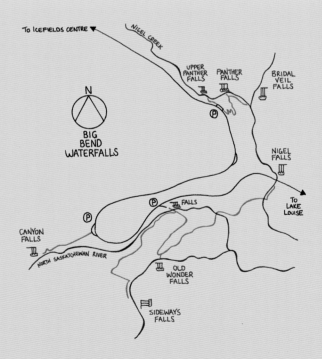

Hiking directions

After parking, walk south along the edge of the vast lot and locate a brown Parks Canada trail sign for Panther Falls and Bridal Veil Falls. The well-used pathway descends from there with views of Bridal Veil Falls through the trees. As you round the final corner, spray from the immense Panther Falls will greet you even before you see the waterfall. The trail continues to descend alongside Nigel Creek until you are below Bridal Veil Falls (Banff National Park, hike #20).

22. Upper Panther Falls

LOCATION: Banff National Park
DRIVING DIFFICULTY: Easy
HIKING DIFFICULTY: Easy
HIKING DISTANCE: 100 m
HIKING TIME: At least 9.87 seconds (current world record for the 100-metre dash)

Driving directions

From the junction of Highway 93 and Highway 11 (Saskatchewan Crossing), drive north on Highway 93 for 36 km to a large, unsigned parking area on the east side of the highway at the top of the "Big Bend."

Hiking directions

Walk to the north end of the parking lot and look for a faint trail leading into the trees. Follow the left-hand side of the creek briefly to a modest but beautiful waterfall. While it pales in comparison to its counterpart just downstream, it is a worthwhile addition to your explorations.

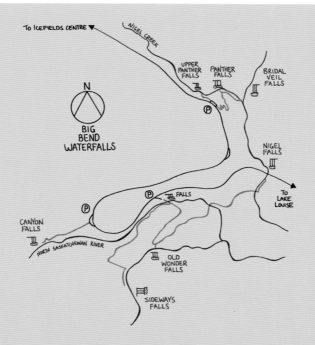

SNAKE INDIAN FALLS
PHOTO: BRIGID SCOTT

CHAPTER 5

More To Explore

The collection of hikes described in this guidebook is by no means an exhaustive list of the waterfalls in the region. While these hikes were compiled primarily with families in mind, there are so many more opportunities to venture into the countless drainages, valleys and watersheds in the Canadian Rockies. Have fun exploring!

A few additional waterfalls, recognizable to some, have been omitted due to overly lengthy approaches, excessive bushwhacking or trail closures at the time of writing. Brief descriptions are included below.

1. FRYATT FALLS – JASPER NATIONAL PARK

Fryatt Falls is a beautiful, large waterfall that tumbles down a steep wall near the headwaters of Fryatt Creek. The trailhead is located 2 km up the Geraldine road (for driving directions see hikes 10 and 11 in Jasper National Park). The hike to the Headwall campground near the base of the falls is 21.5 km one way. An overnight trip is required, with a stay at either the Fryatt, the Brussels or the Headwall campground. The Alpine Club of Canada's Sydney Vallance (Fryatt) Hut is located above the headwall in an alpine basin and used as a basecamp for climbing the peaks high above the Fryatt valley. **Note:** The first 11.7 km of the Fryatt Valley trail can be done on bicycle.

2. SNAKE INDIAN FALLS – JASPER NATIONAL PARK

If we were to publish a book called *Waterfall **Bikes** of the Canadian Rockies*, Snake Indian Falls would be the premier trip. Logistically, this is a tough outing to plan. Job number one is to negotiate the Celestine Lakes road east of Jasper. Travel on this 30 km gravel road is one-way reversible, with specified hours of the day for inbound and outbound traffic; check for schedules. Once at the Celestine Lakes trailhead, hike or bike the trail along the Snake Indian River for 27 km to these spectacular falls. If on foot, this will likely be a multi-day hike, whereas the trip can be dispatched in 5–8 h with a mountain bike.

3. RUBY FALLS – CADOMIN, ALBERTA

Without an ATV or other vehicle capable of stream crossings, a hike to Ruby Falls would be approximately 22 km one way. It's included here not so much to tell you precisely where it is and how to get there, as to simply mention that it exists and is spoken highly of. This is the most remote waterfall referenced in this book and possibly one of the remotest in Alberta. Getting to Cadomin is just half the battle. Best to scope out some online resources and preprogram a route and waypoints into a GPS device.

4. WHITEHORSE CREEK FALLS – CADOMIN, ALBERTA

Another waterfall near the remote town of Cadomin in the front ranges of Alberta's Rockies. The Whitehorse Creek Provincial Recreation Area and campground is 6 km south of Cadomin. The trail starts at the west end of the campground and the distance to the falls is 12 km one-way. The route is popular with equestrian users, so hikers should expect to share the trail with horses.

5. HIDDEN FALLS – YA HA TINDA RANCH, ALBERTA

This waterfall involves a brisk and often sketchy crossing of the Red Deer River near Ya Ha Tinda Ranch. It is generally managed by those on horseback. Otherwise the crossing has to be made later in the summer when the river is low. From the Bighorn campground in Ya Ha Tinda, hike along the north side of the Red Deer River for approximately 5.5 km. Look for a place to ford. Locate a boot-beaten trail leading into a small draw. The waterfall is tucked into a narrow canyon that is about 1.5 km from the river, depending on where you cross. Alternatively, you can cross the river near the campground and follow a horse trail on the south side of the river.

6. TRAPPER'S CREEK WATERFALL – ROCKY MOUNTAIN HOUSE, ALBERTA

Also known locally as Old Town Falls. Park at Riverside Park, just south of Highway 11A on the east side of the North Saskatchewan River. Walk south along the bank of the river for about 400 m, passing under a railway bridge. Turn left to walk up Trapper's Creek, where it is only a short distance farther to the falls.

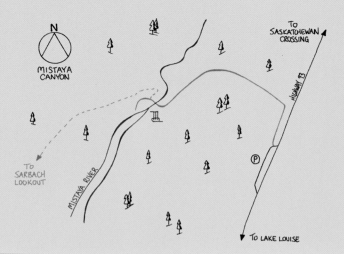

7. MURCHISON FALLS – BANFF NATIONAL PARK

In the category of spectacular and renowned ice climbs is Murchison Falls. While it is briefly visible from the Icefields Parkway, there is no formal summer trail nor is there a parking area. The best vantage point of the falls might be from Sarbach Lookout, across the valley. Sarbach Lookout can be reached via a 5.5 km trail that starts from the Mistaya Canyon trailhead. Cross the bridge over Mistaya Canyon and look for trail signage on the other side of the river. The trail gains 500 m to the location of an old fire lookout.

8. CERBERUS FALLS – BUSH RIVER

This is the double black diamond of all the waterfalls listed in the book. It takes dedication, courage and a supreme effort to visit these waterfalls, and they are generally only seen by mountaineers approaching the Lyell Icefield via the Bush and the Valenciennes rivers. From Golden, drive northwest on the Trans-Canada Highway to Donald and then follow the gravel Bush River Road for 72 km. Just past the Valenciennes River recreation site, turn right, onto the Valenciennes FSR. After 11 km you'll come to where the FSR has been decommissioned. Hike or bike the remnants of the road for the next 13 km, through a series of creeks and significant washouts, to a hairpin turn. From here you can either bushwhack along Icefall Brook into a basin below the falls or access the climbers approach route to view the falls from a bench high above the valley floor. Extensive research is recommended before this undertaking.

9. MOUNT BRYCE FALLS – BUSH RIVER

Perhaps the longest drive on a forestry road you will ever encounter. With driving directions similar to Cerberus Falls above, drive the Bush River Road for approximately 90 km. Cross a bridge over the Bush River and turn right, onto the Rice Brook spur road. This road is steep and generally in a state of disrepair that makes it potentially impassable in a vehicle. Alternatively, you can hike this final 3 km stretch of roadway. At a switchback in the road, a large waterfall pouring down the south face of Mount Bryce is visible, in addition to a couple of others past the Rice Brook canyon. If you've seen every other waterfall in western Canada, this would certainly be a worthy objective. Mount Bryce itself is something to behold, rising over 2500 metres from the valley floor. Note that the condition of resource roads varies greatly throughout the year and they are subject to maintenance by the Ministry of Forests and other stakeholders. Weather also can change road conditions quickly and drastically.

GERALDINE FALLS

Author's Picks

FAVOURITES

Michelle Lakes Waterfall, Banff National Park / Cline River area, AB
Caldron Falls and Caldron Lake, Banff National Park, AB
Stanley Falls and Beauty Creek, Jasper National Park, AB

BEST PICNIC AREAS

Ram Falls, Ram Falls Provincial Park, AB
Cavell Meadows, Jasper National Park
Hargreaves Shelter, Berg Lake, Mount Robson Provincial Park, BC

BEST SWIMMING HOLES

James Falls, Ya Ha Tinda Ranch, AB
Allstones Falls, Cline River area, AB
White Goat Falls, Cline River Area, AB

BEST PLACES TO GET WET

Emperor Falls, Mount Robson Provincial Park, BC
Panther Falls, Banff National Park, AB
Weeping Wall, Banff National Park, AB

BEST DRIVE-UP WATERFALLS (LESS THAN FIVE MINUTES FROM ROAD)

Crescent Falls, Crescent Falls Provincial Recreation Area, AB
Tangle Falls, Jasper National Park, AB
Maligne Canyon Falls, Jasper National Park, AB

BEST "STROLLER-ABLE" FALLS

Crescent Falls, Crescent Falls Provincial Recreation Area, AB
Sunwapta Falls, Jasper National Park, AB
Angel Glacier Falls, Jasper National Park, AB

BEST PLACES TO SPEND A NIGHT

Berg Lake Campground, Mount Robson Provincial Park, BC
Waterfowl Lakes Campground, Banff National Park, AB
Thompson Creek Recreation Area, AB

ANGEL GLACIER FALLS

ENDNOTES

1. "Rearguard Falls Park and salmon," bcparks.ca/explore/parkpgs/ rearguard; **see also** "Where to see the salmon run…, visitvale-mount.ca/where-to-see-the-salmon-run-in-the-valemount-area, accessed 2023-08-29.

2. "A brief history of the Icefields Parkway," pc.gc.ca/en/pn-np/ab/ jasper/activ/itineraires-itineraries/promenadedesglaciers-ice-fieldsparkway/PGhistoire-IPhistory; **see also** "A journey through history – The Icefields Parkway," *Jasper Fitzhugh*, fitzhugh.ca/a-journey-through-history-the-icefields-parkway, both accessed 2023-08-29.

3. "Lord Stanley," thecanadianencyclopedia.ca/en/article/frederick-arthur-stanley-baron-stanley-of-preston-16th-earl-of-derby, ac-cessed 2023-08-29.

4. "Stoney Place Names," Alberta Online Encyclopedia (archived), is.gd/ReGDyx; **see also** "Stories from the Land: Indigenous Place Names in Canada," *RETROactive*, is.gd/UyMBtU, both accessed 2023-08-29.

5. "Banff National Park: Ecosystems and habitat," pc.gc.ca/en/ pn-np/ab/banff/nature/environnement-environment/ecosyste-mes-ecosystems, accessed 2023-08-29.

6. "Nordegg, the name," nordegg.info/History/Nordegg_Name. html; **see also** "Martin Nordegg," archivesalberta.org/2007ex-hibit/jahsena3.htm, both accessed 2023-08-29.

7. "Siffleur," merriam-webster.com/dictionary/siffleur, accessed 2023-08-29.

8. "About Bill Peyto," hihostels.ca/en/about/hostels/bill-peytos-café; **see also** "Bill Peyto, Rocky Mountain Guide and Outfitter," whytemuseum.blogspot.com/2011/05/bill-peyto-rocky-moun-tain-guide-and.html, both accessed 2023-08-29.

9. "The Road to Nowhere," *Vail* (Colorado) *Daily*, vaildaily.com/news/ the-road-to-nowhere, accessed 2023-08-29.

LOWER CONIFER CREEK WATERFALL

REFERENCES

Alberta Online Encyclopedia (archived). "Stoney Place Names." is.gd/ReGDyx, accessed 2023-08-29.

Archives Society of Alberta: JAHSENA. "Martin Nordegg." archive-salberta.org/2007exhibit/jahsena3.htm, accessed 2023-08-29.

BC Parks. "Rearguard Falls Park." bcparks.ca/explore/parkpgs/rearguard, accessed 2023-08-29.

Canadian Encyclopedia, The. "Lord Stanley." thecanadianencyclopedia.ca/en/article/frederick-arthur-stanley-baron-stanley-of-preston-16th-earl-of-derby, accessed 2023-08-29.

Hostelling International Canada. "Bill Peyto's Café: About Bill." hi-hostels.ca/en/about/hostels/bill-peytos-café, accessed 2023-08-29.

Jasper Fitzhugh. "A journey through history – The Icefields Parkway." fitzhugh.ca/a-journey-through-history-the-icefields-parkway, accessed 2023-08-29.

Merriam-Webster.com Dictionary. "Siffleur." merriam-webster.com/dictionary/siffleur, accessed 2023-08-29.

Nordegg.info. "Nordegg, the name." nordegg.info/History/Nordegg_Name.html, accessed 2023-08-29.

Parks Canada. "A brief history of the Icefields Parkway." pc.gc.ca/en/pn-np/ab/jasper/activ/itineraires-itineraries/promenadedesglaciers-icefieldsparkway/PGhistoire-IPhistory, accessed 2023-08-29.

Parks Canada. "Banff National Park: Ecosystems and habitat." pc.gc.ca/en/pn-np/ab/banff/nature/environnement-environment/ecosystemes-ecosystems, accessed 2023-08-29.

RETRO*active*: *Exploring Alberta's Past* (blog). "Stories from the Land: Indigenous Place Names in Canada." is.gd/UyMBtU, accessed 2023-08-29.

Vail (Colorado) *Daily*. "The Road to Nowhere." vaildaily.com/news/the-road-to-nowhere, accessed 2023-08-29.

Whyte Museum of the Canadian Rockies: *Peaks and People* (blog). "Bill Peyto, Rocky Mountain Guide and Outfitter." whytemuseum.blogspot.com/2011/05/bill-peyto-rocky-mountain-guide-and.html, accessed 2023-08-29.

CRESCENT FALLS

ONLINE RESOURCES

Alberta Parks – trail search and conditions, reservations
albertaparks.ca

Alberta Motor Association – Alberta road conditions
roadreports.ama.ab.ca

Alpine Club of Canada – backcountry hut bookings
alpineclubofcanada.ca/how-to-book/

BC Parks – park name search and reservations
bcparks.ca/find-a-park/
bcparks.ca/reservations/

Drive BC – British Columbia road conditions
drivebc.ca

Recreation Sites and Trails BC
gov.bc.ca/gov/content/sports-culture/recreation/camping-hiking/
sites-trails

Parks Canada – trail conditions, park pass information, reservations
pc.gc.ca/en/index

Leave No Trace
leavenotrace.ca

Wildsafe BC
wildsafebc.com

PARK VISITOR CENTRES

Mount Robson Provincial Park
bcparks.ca/mount-robson-park
Hwy 16, Mount Robson, BC,
V0E 2Z0
250-566-4038
Camping reservations:
1-800-689-9025 from Canada
and US
1-519-858-6161 internationally
camping.bcparks.ca

Jasper National Park
parks.canada.ca/pn-np/ab/jasper
500 Connaught Dr, Jasper, AB
780-852-6176
Camping reservations:
1-877-737-3783

1-519-826-5391 outside
North America

David Thompson Country
davidthompsoncountry.ca,
with contact links to visitor
centres in Rocky Mountain
House, Caroline, Nordegg and
Clearwater County

Banff National Park
parks.canada.ca/pn-np/ab/Banff
224 Banff Avenue, Banff, AB
403-762-1550
Camping reservations:
parks.canada.ca/pn-np/ab/banff/
activ/camping

SECOND SIFFLEUR FALLS

Index of Waterfalls

Other Titles by Steve Tersmette

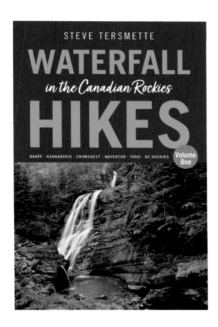 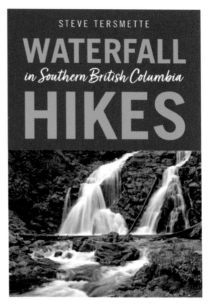

**WATERFALL HIKES IN
THE CANADIAN ROCKIES**
Volume 1

**Banff • Kananaskis
Crowsnest • Waterton
Yoho • BC Rockies**

Steve Tersmette
9781771606165

**WATERFALL HIKES IN
SOUTHERN BRITISH COLUMBIA**

Steve Tersmette
9781771604277

STEVE TERSMETTE was introduced to the mountains by his parents at a young age and grew up hiking and backpacking in the Canadian Rockies. In 2006 he moved to Kimberley, where he continues to explore the mountains with his friends, wife, and two young children. In 2017, along with his best friend and climbing partner, he became the first to traverse the Purcell Mountains on foot in the summer by trekking from near Kimberley to Rogers Pass. Steve is also an avid climber and mountaineer and has established first ascents and new climbing routes in both the Purcells and the Rockies. He actively volunteers with the East Kootenay Climbing Association to advocate for, maintain, and develop outdoor climbing in southeastern BC. He lives in Kimberley, British Columbia.